A Champion of Good

A Champion of Good

The Life of Father Ilarion

Natalia Mikhailovna Kopyttseva
Translated by Nathan K. Williams

Holy Trinity Publications
The Printshop of St Job of Pochaev
Holy Trinity Monastery
Jordanville, New York
2011

Printed with the blessing of His Eminence,
Metropolitan Hilarion First Hierarch
of the Russian Orthodox Church Outside of Russia

HOLY TRINITY PUBLICATIONS
The Printshop of St Job of Pochaev
Holy Trinity Monastery
Jordanville, New York 13361-0036
www.holytrinitypublications.com

ISBN: 978-0-88465-189-5 (paper)
ISBN: 978-0-88465-207-6 (ePub)

Library of Congress Control Number 2011936945

CONTENTS

PREFACE TO THE ENGLISH LANGUAGE EDITION

I am an American Orthodox Christian and was raised in Ter-ryville, Connecticut. Since 1994, I have served in Russia on a number of expatriate assignments. In 1996, I took a job that brought my family and me to Veliky Novgorod, and it was not long before I received a very nice letter asking to help with the Bronnitsa church school. My wife Nadia and I went to check out the school, which is where we met Father Ilarion.

It did not take much time to realize that this was the spiritual father we both had been looking for. Not only was Father Ilarion such a perfect example of what you would imagine a strong, spiritual, and wise father to be, but also he was very easy to approach and ask advice on any subject. We immediately became his "kids" and visited him on a regular basis. His advice, and sometimes cryptic predictions about our lives, my career, and people we knew, all came true, one by one.

Shortly after we became acquainted with Father Ilarion, his health began to deteriorate. He then made a pilgrimage to Jerusalem, which was his lifelong dream. The spiritual inspiration he received from this trip seemed to have added another ten years to his life, and for that, we are very grateful. Those additional ten years of advice, wisdom, and, most importantly, his prayers have helped guide us through all the trials and tribulations which life sometimes presents.

In January 2000, I took a new job, which brought my family and me back to St Petersburg, approximately 112 miles away from

Veliky Novgorod. Yet, we always made time to visit Father Ilarion at least once per quarter and always celebrated Pascha with him, both in church and at his dinner table in his humble house after the midnight service was completed. Even when his health was failing, and he had trouble eating, he still insisted that we sit at his table. As you would expect, we had many questions for him about life, the future, and always some new problem or issue we were dealing with. Father Ilarion smiled and patiently took on these problems, and through his prayers, one by one, the problems were solved, and the future revealed itself just as he predicted.

Father Ilarion was a perfect example of how to live like a Christian in a modern world that seems devoid of good Christian examples. He could talk about the Bible to simple village people, and also be the designated confessor for all priests in the Novgorod Diocese. He was strict and loving at the same time. If he knew you were upset with something he said, even if you deserved it, it bothered him tremendously, and he would immediately ask your forgiveness until it was given. In reality, it was ourselves and our pride that caused the problem, and it should have been us asking his forgiveness!

Many of the Glinsk Monastery elders who lived with Father Ilarion during his early monastic years have now been canonized by the Ukrainian Orthodox Church, and I have no doubt that Father Ilarion will soon join their ranks.

Philip Wegh

FROM THE PREFACE TO THE RUSSIAN LANGUAGE EDITION

In Prayerful Memory, with Heartfelt Love and Gratitude

The day our dear Father Ilarion reposed was one of profound drama for us. We had lost a spiritual father, an elder, a person whom we

Thou didst create us for Thyself, and our heart hath no peace until it findeth rest in Thee![1]

could neither fully understand nor comprehend with our hearts. Yet, although deprived of direct spiritual, soulful communion with him, we must be fully conscious of his place in our hearts, which nothing and no one can fill, of his spiritual strength, and of his profound concern for each person who ever entered the church or approached him at any time.

All of us who grieve for Father Ilarion realize and sense that in departing this life, he did not take with him the many riches of his spiritual person, but rather left them to us, multiplying our love for him, and confirming in us the belief that there is no death! Father lives, and he is with us. Just as the Glinsk vigil lamp illuminated and warmed the souls of the brethren of and pilgrims to the Glinsk Monastery, the flame that illuminated Father's face and soul, for he was and is truly illumined, is a beacon that shines to all of us through the darkness of monotony, warming hearts and continuing to warm them, burning up sins, and accomplishing the wonder of liberating souls from sin through sincere repentance.

Our faith in God and our love for Father Ilarion was a spiritual font, filling our souls with consolation and the joyous hope of an assured future reunion with him. It is this that inspired the desire to compile everything concerning him, everything that reminds us of him, everything that helps us feel and experience his presence with us and our mutual prayerful intimacy. Naturally, Father's inner life and spiritual labors were hidden from us, his spiritual children and parishioners. We could only see individual deeds and hear words that determined our subsequent life's pathways, everything that would show up as though by chance, for our spiritual benefit.

Father did not like to be admired and always cut off with a joke anyone expressing admiration for him. It is not for us to determine the merits or faults of the people around us, especially the clergy; "But he who is spiritual judges all things, yet he himself is rightly judged by no one."[2] Judgment and praise are for God alone. However, on the basis of official documents, the recollections of eyewitnesses, and the living word of Father's preaching, both from the ambon in the church and in private conversation with his spiritual children, and as preserved in his many notebooks and in audio recordings and letters, we can and must bear witness to what could not be hidden from those around him. As his physical image fades from our souls, we must give readers the opportunity to better know the spiritual image of the elder whose prayers securely defended us from the powers of darkness, and who to this day cares for us, praying for us before the throne of God, and helping each of us valiantly bear his cross along the thorny road of life.

We express our deep gratitude to our benefactors: Nadezhda and Philip Wegh, A. Galov, A. A. Mukharev, O. V. and T. A. Surkov, N. B. Akhundov, N. S. Chistyakov, and others.

It would be impossible to name all the people who responded with love, rendering spiritual, moral, and material support in bringing this publication to fruition. All who took part in creating this book constantly felt the prayerful aid of our ever-memorable Father Ilarion, without which this book would never have gone to press.

Who shall separate us from the love of Christ? Shall tribulation, or distress, or persecution, or famine, or nakedness, or peril, or sword? . . . Yet in all these things we are more than conquerors through Him who loved us. For I am persuaded that neither death nor life, nor angels nor principalities nor powers, nor things present nor things to come, nor height nor depth, nor any other created thing, shall be able to separate us from the love of God which is in Christ Jesus our Lord.[4]

It is heartening to note that its release coincides with three memorable dates: the eighty-fifth anniversary of Father's birth, the thirty-fifth anniversary of his clerical service in Novgorod, and the 1,150th anniversary of Veliky Novgorod.

I was Father Ilarion's spiritual child for fifteen years and would not have dared undertake the task if Father himself had not blessed me to work on his archive, and if the work had not received a hierarchal blessing. With a sense of profound reverence, fear of God, and consciousness of my own unworthiness, I began the work of formulating the material entrusted to me and compiling my personal recollections of our dear, memorable Father. I seek justification for my boldness in the mercy of God and in my love for Father Ilarion.

We ask God for His blessing on this labor, and you, brothers and sisters, for your prayers. "The righteous will be in everlasting remembrance."[3]

Throughout the year following Father Ilarion's death, at the end of the liturgy, a hymn based on these words was sung. It resonated in the hearts of Father Ilarion's spiritual children, who saw him literally melt away before their eyes. The hymn sounded a piercing note not only of parting from him, but also in confirmation that nothing can separate us from Father, that not even pitiless death itself can tear us away from love for our beloved, and that neither death nor anything or anyone else can tear the believing Christian away from the love of God.

> In our day also God doth raise up
> Champions of good in our midst,
> Through them reminding, in manifold ways:
> The beacon of faith doth persist.[5]

Divine providence was profoundly evident both in Father Ilarion's birth on the great day of the Nativity of the honorable and glorious prophet and forerunner John, the Baptizer of the Lord, who called the people to repentance, and in Father's repose forty days before the same memorable date. Father Ilarion's own theological writings are dedicated to the subject of repentance, and along with his preaching, are seen as a testament left to his spiritual children: "Repent, for the kingdom of heaven is at hand! . . . Prepare the way of the Lord, make His paths straight."[6]

Natalia Mikhailovna Kopyttseva

PART I

LIFE

CHAPTER I

From Infancy to Monastic Rebirth

Archimandrite Ilarion (Ivan Fomich Prikhodko in the world) was born on June 24/July 7, 1924, in the village of Alenovka in the Unecha Region, to a pious peasant family and was given the name Ivan.

His father, Foma Petrovich, was a strict but fair man. His mother, Iuliana Petrovna, a simple, kind country woman, was a prudent, humble person. "Forgive me, forgive me, forgive me," her brief conversations with anyone would conclude. She spoke and acted in the spirit of the old saying, "measure twice, cut once." Before saying or doing anything, she would think for a long time, and for this reason, she was almost never mistaken. Her authority in the family was absolute, and her influence on her son's spiritual upbringing and path in life may be considered to have been decisive. As Mother Varvara of Pinsk recalled, monasticism was offered to Ivan's mother, but she declined, considering herself unworthy. Father Ilarion frequently recalled her with profound love and gratitude, both in his private conversations and his sermons.

There were three children in the family: a daughter, Efrosinia, and two sons. Dmitry, six years Ivan's senior, was killed during the Germans' retreat from Bryansk in 1944 when he was 26, leaving two children. When he was killed, the clairvoyant Mother Evlampia, who lived in a neighboring village, had a dream in which she saw him dead. She visited the family, and Ivan went to her. Their meeting proved a fateful one for him. "Happy is the mother who has such a son," she said at the time to Iuliana Petrovna, "and happy is the son who has such a mother." Later, a warning she gave him would save Ivan from death in the war.

As a child, Vanya, as they called him, was a candid, guileless boy. Once, when his sister had misbehaved, in answer to his father's stern, inquiring glance, he replied, "Papa, I would tell you today that Bronka [as they called her at home] broke the glass, but you'd get angry, so I'd better tell you tomorrow." Father remained just as childishly simplehearted to the end of his days. One could not unobtrusively complain to him of someone else in private, for he would clear up the situation on the spot without delay. "Come here for a minute!" he would say. "She says that you said [or did] such and such. Is this true?" This method of resolving a conflict at its inception permanently squelched the desire of any "do-gooders" to snitch on their neighbors.

Following the example of his parents, particularly his mother, the boy grew up to be quite pious. He prayed to God, shunned worldly vanity, and fervently visited the temple of God. Vanya was very neat and hard working. Together, he and his sister would clean the house, prepare meals, and keep the yard tidy. Later on, his cell in the Glinsk Monastery was always clean and in order, the bed neatly made without a single wrinkle, and the floor clean without a speck of dust. His cell in Bronnitsa was just as impeccable.

Vanya studied well and, from childhood, possessed an excellent memory: while his sister was still learning a poem, he would already be reciting it. All these virtues, thanks to wise guidance, would receive their future development in the monastery.

For a time, they lived well and prospered, but the new Soviet policies brought drastic changes to Alenovka and its inhabitants. The family was dispossessed, and their land and livestock were seized. Much later, in one of his sermons, Father recalled, "My father never hired anyone to work for him and exploited no one. Yet, they stripped us of everything, trimming us right to the bone, because we had something that they did not. And who were they? The proletariat of all countries, the poor who did not want to work for their daily bread—these people were only capable of devouring what belonged to others." All were driven into the collective farms. The Prikhodko family, however, did not join one of these, as Iuliana Petrovna remained categorically opposed to what she considered a godless way of treating peasant farming.

Ivan was born with a fine voice and a good ear for music, and he loved to sing. His father bought him a balalaika, which he quickly mastered and played constantly. As he grew up, he became more and more handsome and well built, with thick, wavy, pitch-black hair. The girls followed the boy, and later the young man, in droves.

Heaven looked after its chosen one, however. Ivan went to a dance hall only once. When he returned home, he told his mother, "I'll never go to a dance again. The Archangel Michael told me not to!" This was God's call, offering him the straight and narrow path of monasticism in place of dances, parties, and other adolescent pleasures. One sign of this was when, just before Nativity, the sixteen-year-old boy saw the Star of Bethlehem in the sky. That was something to think about!

Life was not easy. Ivan had to earn money for bread and to help his parents. He took any work he could find, unloading railroad cars, painting, and the like. Then, war broke out.

The Germans occupied Bryansk Region and encamped in Alenovka. They seized everything that had been left on the family's farm after the Soviet government had exacted its toll. Ivan's mother worked from morning to night, weaving and sewing. Meanwhile, he wove bast shoes, maintained the roof, and spaded and weeded the garden. The Germans nearly took the young man off to Germany. He escaped this, however, with the help of kind people who obtained a note from a local doctor, citing an allegedly injured eye. Of course, it was prayers that helped first and foremost: his own and his mother's.

Like all the young men his age, Ivan left for the front in 1943, where one of his fellow soldiers promptly "assigned himself" to him: the fellow informed on Ivan constantly, reporting that he was hiding a cross, praying on the sly, and so forth. The unit commander, however, turned out to be a decent person. He had great respect for young Ivan and supported him, although he did explain that, due to Ivan's faith, he was destined to remain a perpetual soldier. In those days, a believer could only be a private, not an officer. Within half a year of his arrival to the front, Ivan suffered a severe wound and was sent to the hospital. While there, he met two Orthodox servants of the Catacomb Church: the nuns Pavlina and Evlampia.[1]

War opened the young man's eyes to the horrific lie that permeated the Soviet regime, and he returned to the clear, simple truths his parents had taught him. Later, Father Ilarion recalled, "God's grace touched my heart, and my heart was inflamed by the Lord. And neither lofty words nor arguments and proofs were necessary anymore."[2] No doubts remained as to his monastic path, although the road would not be a smooth one. Upon his return home, Mother Evlampia told the young soldier that to the end of his earthly days, he must give thanks to God that he had returned from the war alive (she had seen him on the brink of death) and that he would yet save many from the darkness of unbelief and despair.[3]

Ivan began to pay regular visits to the Glinsk Hermitage. When he first arrived, as Mother Valentina recalled him saying, Father Gabriel[4] told him, "You will be ours." Ivan's mother blessed him to enter the monastery and went to live there herself, working at the guesthouse for pilgrims. His father wanted very much for his beloved son to be like everyone else, to marry and give him grandchildren. To have his son enter the Glinsk Hermitage was a heavy blow. He died early, without having seen his son a monk.

CHAPTER 2

At the Glinsk Hermitage:
"A Monastery in the World"

For centuries, our countrymen saw the Glinsk Hermitage as the embodiment of the highest Christian asceticism and moral fortitude. The mere mention of its name spiritually invigorated men's hearts, inflaming them with zeal for salvation. Along with the Kiev Caves and Trinity-Sergius Lavra, the Glinsk Hermitage promoted the common national work of spiritual enlightenment and was a kind of university of eldership in Russia.

One circumstance that influenced the Glinsk Hermitage's particular status compared to other monasteries was the presence of the Glinsk Hermitage wonder-working icon of the Nativity of the Most-Holy Mother of God that appeared there and the many miraculous healings performed through it to the glory of the Mother of God and the strengthening of the Orthodox faith. This drew pious pilgrims from all over the great Russian land. In fact, the monastery's establishment is linked to the appearance on this spot of the wonder-working image of the Mother of God, which was found in the early sixteenth century.

People began to flock to the place of the icon's appearance, not only laymen but also monks, who labored in fasting and prayer. Thus, not far from Putivl (106 miles from Kursk), overshadowed by the wonder-working icon of the Nativity of the Most-Holy Mother of God, the Glinsk Hermitage was established in the sixteenth century. Grace-imbued help from the wonder-working image of the Glinsk Hermitage poured out on everyone and at all times until September 1922, when the Glinsk Hermitage was closed by the new government. Since then, all trace of the monastery's greatest sacred treasure has been lost amid decades of chaos.

According to the prophecies of spiritual elders, the Glinsk Hermitage's wonder-working icon of the Nativity of the Most-Holy Mother of God will appear in this holy monastery as a sign of the rebirth of the Glinsk Monastery, its subsequent prosperity, and the restoration of its significance for the spiritual life of the people. Yet, even hidden from human eyes, the grace-imbued might of the wonder-working image unquestionably continues to pour forth abundantly on all who call on the aid of the Queen of Heaven with true faith of soul and purity of heart. For, as the Holy Hierarch Ignatius (Brianchaninov) rightly stated, "icons of the Mother of God work wonders throughout all the land, preaching, testifying, and sealing with signs the truth of the teaching of Christ."

————————— ◆ —————————

[The Glinsk Hermitage] is a school of Christ: it is one of the bright spots on the globe, which should be entered by first reducing oneself to Christ-like infancy.[1]

————————— ◆ —————————

In ancient times, monasteries were to be found throughout the entire Russian land, for monasticism is the heart of Orthodoxy. By the time of Ivan Prikhodko's arrival at the Glinsk Hermitage, however, it was the only monastery open in Russia. Many, including believers, were not even aware of its existence. There were periods when its material welfare suffered and when the authorities shut down this hated "hotbed of obscurantism." The monastery's spiritual life, however, never grew cold. Located far from human eyes, separated from the world by forests and fields, the Glinsk Hermitage was the ideal place for great spiritual ascetics to lay down their life in service to God and men. Venerable Seraphim of Sarov called the Glinsk Hermitage "a great school of the spiritual life," while Archbishop Yuvenaly (Polovtsev) called it "the ideal of worship and a place of spiritual feats of labor."

Father Ilarion first came to the monastery in 1950, which we know from a certificate that Hierodeacon Ilarion was required to obtain after the hermitage was closed, while trying to determine his future spiritual path. He was unable to stay here for long, however, because his papers had been lost. In time, the Glinsk elders succeeded in resolving this issue, and he was finally accepted into the Glinsk Hermitage, by his own account, in 1955.

It should be noted that the young novice was embarking on the monastic path, choosing a path of service to the Church, at a time when a future as a cleric held nothing for him but the heavy cross of a confessor and martyr, and that he never wavered in his decision. On the contrary, he often regretted that he had not remained in the monastery, although he could not fail to realize that, apparently, such was the will of God for him to be a monk in the world, a servant of the lesser brethren. He believed that He who had laid upon him the burden of sacred service would strengthen him and set him on the right way.

The monastery opened once again in 1942, but its light shone for only nineteen years, until 1961. The war and postwar years were very hard, and the monastery lacked for everything: building materials, food, and clothing. The brethren wore bast shoes, baked bread that was half flour and half potato, and at times ate nothing but beets in place of bread.

When the future Archimandrite Ilarion arrived at the monastery, however, the hermitage was in its prime. To be sure, its outward appearance remained unsightly. There remained the eastern wall, the monastery tower, the hierarchal building containing the bishop's house, and the church, dedicated to the Feast of the Exaltation of the Cross of the Lord. Upon exiting the church, one immediately found oneself in a long corridor with cells located along both sides.

On the common beside the church stood a lamppost bearing a kerosene lamp or candle. A little to the west of the lamppost stood the so-called Moscow Lodge: one part of it was inhabited by the monks, another part housed a medical station, and a corner room served as the guest room for "capitol guests," Muscovites and Leningraders who were primarily doctors. When many people were visiting, the floor of the common cell was furnished with mattresses and pillows stuffed with hay.

Despite the outward poverty, however, the spiritual life in the hermitage was on such a high level that, according to an eminent Glinsk elder, Master of Theology Schema-Archimandrite Ioann (Maslov, ✝ 1991), the divine services served by its pastors "gave rebirth to the souls of sinners and turned them to God." The sentiment of those who came to pray there, according to Father Ioann, could be expressed thus: "We felt there as though we were among the saints, and we walked with fear as though in the Holy Land."[2]

Here, a perpetual vigil lamp burned, the gleam of which beckoned like stars in the night to all those suffering and laden with sins and concerns. Pilgrims flocked from all over Russia to its perpetual light, to the monastery's God-pleasing hospitality, braving the difficult journey with its transfers and many trials. The pilgrims brought an ardent desire to help in the monastery's restoration, along with food, clothing, and other goods. All were met with joy and provided lodging. They were given three days to rest, acclimate to the long services, and confess. Then, the visitors were blessed to begin work. With the help of such benefactors, a farmyard was set up, a forge was rebuilt on the site of the previous one, a new refectory was constructed, and so forth.

The light of Christ illuminated and enlightened everyone and everything in the Glinsk Hermitage. It would become indelibly imprinted on the faces of the monastery's inhabitants, who were scattered throughout the country after its closing. It was this light that always shone in the face of our dear Father Ilarion, whose very name in Greek means quiet and joyous. This name given to him in monasticism was most appropriate to that steady, unflickering flame that always burned in his heart, as a sign of the profound dedication of this chosen one of God to the instructions of his spiritual fathers and to Glinsk Hermitage, so memorable, so dear to his heart, and so delightful.

The Glinsk elders lovingly took the young brother under their spiritual care, and one of them, Archimandrite Seraphim (Romantsov), became his spiritual father. By this time, the holy hermitage was home to several dozen brethren. (For comparison, between 1942–1952, more than one hundred and thirty people joined the hermitage, whilst between 1953–1958, forty-eight people joined.) In 1950, the monastery brethren numbered sixty-four, of whom monks over age sixty comprised seventy percent, of whom twenty-six were disabled.[3] At the time of his entry into the monastery, Father Ilarion was thirty-one years old.

At the end of the 1940s, nearly all of the older generation of the monastery brethren had returned from exile and imprisonment. Some of them had lived in the hermitage prior to its closing in 1922. They formed a council of elders, which decided all vital issues. "Strict with himself, the pious father superior Archimandrite Seraphim keeps a sharp eye on the behavior of all the novices, and permits no one to depart in any way from the rules of the monastic life."

During Father Ilarion's time at the monastery, the nucleus of its spiritual life consisted of Archimandrite Seraphim (Amelin), Schema-Hegumen Andronik (Lukash), and Hieroschemamonk Seraphim (Romantsov). Through their labors, the Glinsk Hermitage waxed strong and prospered. Under their guidance, "a host of ascetics" grew up, many of whom, inheriting their spirit, later spread the Glinsk Hermitage traditions of eldership throughout the land.

The young, newly arrived novice was given a cell with Brother Vlasy (Vasily Mikhailovich Sumin in the world, 1897–1989).[4] A brief letter of greeting from Brother Vlasy has survived. Like Father Ilarion, Brother Vlasy grew up in a peasant family. He entered the Glinsk Hermitage in 1953, after returning from twenty years' exile in the Chelyabinsk camps, and was ordained a hieromonk a year later.

The monastery brethren performed obediences of every kind. At first, the novice Ivan performed coenobitic obediences, going daily to the elder, who was the bedrock of spiritual monastic life in the monastery, to reveal his thoughts, learning to pray and labor in complacent endurance of sorrows and fasting, heeding the teachings of the monastery superior, strictly controlling his thoughts and feelings, and reading the works of the Holy Fathers. The monastery strictly observed the rule established by Abbot Philaret (Davilevsky) in the nineteenth century, modeled after the Athonite rule. The monks had no personal possessions, and the brethren performed all menial labor themselves. Women were not admitted, except into the church, and relatives were permitted to visit the monks with the superior's blessing only in the guest room, as visitation in the cells was not permitted.

There was no electricity, as it was considered an unnecessary luxury, or plumbing. There was a well on the property from which the novices pumped water throughout the day. Several people lived in each cell. They prayed secretly, and many would spend the night standing in prayer; in the summertime, they would go down to the basement to pray. The food was of the very simplest sort: cabbage soup, porridge, and the like. Fish was served once a year. At meals, they read from the Holy Fathers: Anthony the Great, John of the Ladder, Abba Dorotheus, Isaac the Syrian, Ephraim the Syrian, Theophan the Recluse, Holy Hierarch Ignatius (Brianchaninov), and others. The works of these ascetics later became the favorite reading material of Father Ilarion and his spiritual children. There was a fine library with many spiritual books, which both monks and pilgrims could receive a blessing to read.

After four years of life in the monastery, in 1959, the novice Ivan's true monastic intentions being evident, he was tonsured a rasophore with the name Ilarion, in honor of Venerable Ilarion the Great. Two years later, in 1961, he was elevated to the rank of hieromonk with the same name.[5] On the door of his cell appeared the framed inscription "Hieromonk Ilarion."

Having taken his place at the church altar, Father Ilarion gave himself up wholly and entirely to pastoral work. That for which his soul had hungrily longed in patient expectation of God's will had finally come to pass. Father Ilarion related how, after his tonsure to the mantle, he felt such an unprecedented influx of spiritual energy, and a life filled with such ineffable joy. Such hitherto unknown spiritual enjoyment was opened to him that for the first few months, he felt as if he was flying among the clouds. Throughout his life, he acutely remembered the great day of his tonsure and the vows that he then took.

It is not given to us weak ones to penetrate the mysteries of monastic feats and labors. They are seen by the one Knower of hearts and are comprehensible to those who fight the good fight. For our part, we are edified by the deeds of the young monk, which he performed in the sight of the Glinsk brethren around him. Abbot Philaret wrote, "From the depths of their solitude, true monks shine forth upon the world by their simple, God-pleasing way of life and their living, active words of saving truth."[6]

Life in the hermitage was strict, and there was almost no free time outside of obediences. The monastery superior, Father Seraphim (Amelin), assigned the monk Ilarion to the post of letter writer. His duty was to send edifying answers to the multitudinous letters that came to the monastery, and letters of thanks to those who sent donations, packages, and lists of names for commemoration. In addition, having noted early on the young novice's voice and love of church singing, the monastic administration later appointed him to the post of choir director.

Perceiving the young monk's remarkable abilities and zeal for piety, the superior blessed him to receive visitors who came seeking advice. Word of his spiritual wisdom spread quickly among the pilgrims. Nun Barbara (Vera Feodorovna Gashicheva in the world), who came from Bryansk in 2008 to accompany Father Ilarion to his final resting place, recalled, "Our Bryansk people advised me to travel to the Glinsk Hermitage to the deacon Ilarion, and I went. Despite the fact that there were elders there, many went to the young deacon Ilarion. He scheduled services of needs. He lived in one cell with Fr Vlasy. He also had a separate reception room for scheduling the forty-day prayers for the departed, the reading of the Psalter, and so forth. So I began coming to visit Fr Ilarion. When they closed the Glinsk Hermitage, I helped him move his belongings."[7]

People came to the Glinsk Hermitage from various cities to ask Father Ilarion for advice and instruction. His talks with the elders served to channel into him that grace-imbued state with which he would be filled after many years in monastic labors and, through conversation with him, was passed on to the people around him. It is for this state, of an internal spiritual monastery and for its establishment in the souls of others, that his soul would always yearn.

In the cell of the superior, Father Seraphim, there was an icon of the Hebron Mother of God, which the monastery's spiritual transformer, Abbot Philaret (Danilevsky), brought to the monastery as a blessing in 1817. According to tradition, on the day of his arrival at the monastery, a new swarm of bees joined the apiary, which the monks took as a blessing from God. Father Ilarion always particularly revered the image of the Hebron Mother of God, which adorns the first row of the iconostas in the Bronnitsa church.[8]

An icon ardently revered in the Glinsk church was the Image of the Savior Not-Made-By-Human-Hands, which someone had preserved in the years of ruination. According to local tradition, before the monastery's first devastation, it had stood in the cell of one of the monks and possessed an amazing quality: the minute any of those in the cell began to speak idly, a crack would be heard. The monks knew of this and had to consider it seriously by moderating their speech. Incidentally, Father Ilarion was not loquacious and always cut off the talkative by saying, "This is all vain talking, idle talking." He instructed people to avoid idle talking and remember to pray instead.

One woman pilgrim to Glinsk in the 1950s recalled, "In the church itself everything was very simple and ... clean.... The iconostas was three-tiered. In the local tier, the life-size icons of the Mother of God and the Savior beneath metal icon shields were the only ones that matched. All the others had been collected from various places and differed in content, style, and school. No one minded in the least."[9] The elders loved to say, "Where simplicity dwells, a hundred angels fly, but where fancy flies no angel dwells."

The Glinsk Hermitage came to life well before dawn, around four o'clock. By six o'clock, when the Midnight Office was being read, the sun was already streaming into the altar. At Matins, the Prologue was read, followed by something from the patristic teachings. The pilgrims listened sitting on the floor, while the monks sat on special wooden seats, called *stasidias*, which stood along the walls. (The kathismata were also listened to while sitting.) After

Matins ended, around eight o'clock, the akathist to the Savior was solemnly chanted. On Saturdays, the akathist to the Mother of God was sung. On a low table in the middle of the church lay a copy of the wonder-working icon of the Nativity of the Most-Holy Mother of God, which was particularly revered in the monastery. At the end of the services the brethren would approach it two by two in order of seniority, followed by all the pilgrims.

At nine o'clock began the Divine Liturgy, which ended around eleven o'clock, but the chanting in the church did not stop. Molebens with akathists were read by request, frequently almost right up to the beginning of Vespers at four o'clock in the evening. Those who remained at the moleben to the very end would miss the meal. The others—first the brethren, then the pilgrims—were invited to the meal, during which they listened to readings from the Holy Fathers. On the evening before communing, it was the custom to not attend the meal; the communicant contented himself with dry foods and hot water.

Vespers was served from four to five o'clock, after which there was a short break. The brethren ate a light repast in their cells, while the pilgrims ate whatever and wherever God sent them. At six o'clock Compline began. Three canons were always read, followed by prayers before sleep. The evening service ended with the monastic rule: to the singing of the stichera to the cross ("We who are guarded by the Cross do oppose the enemy"), the monks would approach the cross by twos and ask one another's forgiveness.

On Sundays and holy days, the services were particular festive. The following is an account from a Glinsk pilgrim of that period:

> Changes could already be seen the evening before: after the hour-long Small Vespers, served from four to five o'clock in the evening, the All-Night Vigil began. People were summoned to the Vigil by an unpretentious "bell tower" hung with pieces of metal of every kind, from which the bell-ringer, using a wrench, would produce a melody fully suited to the occasion. The Hours (for example, the First Hour) were read at one in the morning, and the people left the service in complete darkness, which the solitary lantern set on a

post did little to dissipate. The stars were high above, and one had to adjust to their light to make out which door was the right one, but everyone was together and there was nowhere to become lost. The next morning one could get up a little later than usual—the service began at six o'clock. It included the festal or Sunday Midnight Office, a festive akathist to the Mother of God, the Hours, and Liturgy.

On ordinary days we had to stand at the morning rule from four to six o'clock. When the nursing home loudspeaker awoke, and the strains of *"Reve Ta Stogne"*[10] drifted across the entire territory, we would go to our "obediences." Only the pilgrims who were new arrivals remained in the church. . . .

In the church, people stood reverently, quietly. They tried to whisper when talking, and only asked questions if they needed something. If someone did get carried away and forget themselves, Fr Ioanniky, the tall monk behind the candle desk, would rap on the wooden counter with a pencil. Everyone understood, and conversations ceased.[11]

Metropolitan Zinovy (Mazhuga) related how, when he came to the Glinsk Monastery, "there were still monks living there who knew the New Testament and the Psalter by heart. One of them, a blind chanter, read the Epistle daily at the Liturgy from memory."[12]

As noted above, one of Hieromonk Ilarion's obediences was singing in the choir. He sang the first tenor part and could hit very high notes. After straining his voice, the doctors forbade him to sing, to avoid losing his voice completely. Only a year later, his voice was restored.

As Vera Sholokhova, a parishioner from Orsha, Belarus, recalled,

I met Father Ilarion through the handmaid of God Galina at the Glinsk Hermitage. I was there for the feast of the Nativity of John the Forerunner in 1960. Vladyka (the bishop) came to serve, and there were many people there. Father Ilarion was a hierodeacon. And when he began to cense the church before the Liturgy, the mentally ill people yelled out across the whole church, and jumped on the cathedra. The grace there was very strong. There were clairvoyant monks there. For instance, Fr Feodosy, the sexton, discerned my name, my illness, and where I was born.

Father Ilarion was still directing the choir. The monks at the Glinsk Hermitage sang beautifully. Father had a wonderful voice.

I also met Fr Ilarion during his visit to the Pskov Caves Monastery, during his studies at the Leningrad Theological Academy. There were always many people waiting to confess to him. He taught us to be in the temple for all the services.

Nun Eufemia of the Snetogorsk Monastery recounted how Father Ilarion was considerate of all of the pilgrims, even those he had not yet met:

> I came to know Father in 1961. It was at the Glinsk Hermitage. He summoned me to the monastery through a certain girl (though he had never seen me before). "Write to her," he said, "and have her come. Otherwise she will perish."
>
> I came immediately. Father called me into his cell, gave me many small icons, and for some reason immediately gave me his photograph.
>
> Father was clairvoyant. I could hide no thought, no feeling from him; he would immediately rebuke me. When my mother died, he immediately began to read the funeral dirge and told me to return home as quickly as possible. When I arrived, the priest and the choir were waiting for me to take the coffin away to the cemetery.

After eleven years at the Glinsk Hermitage, Father was sent to serve in Stary Oskol, Belgorod Region. Mother Valentina (Bondarenko) recalled that Father Ilarion spent time there with the novice Alexei, who revealed much to him regarding both the present and the future. In the early 1990s, when he was visiting that city, Father visited the blessed monk Alexei.

Hard times began for the Church in the late 1950s, however. By the early 1960s, the war on religion in the country was at its peak. The Soviet leader Nikita Khrushchev promised to show the world the last Russian priest by 1980 and promised everyone immortality through science by the year 2000. Not only living the life of the

Church but even thinking about it was now prohibited. Believers were declared insane and either imprisoned or exiled. The godless authorities categorically replaced spiritual values with their phantom communist ideology, which within three decades, would crumble to dust.

Naturally, the elders anticipated the closing of the Glinsk Hermitage, yet recalled what Metropolitan Nikolai of Krutitsk and Kolomensk had said to them: "While I live, the Glinsk Hermitage will not be closed."[13] As the chairman of the Foreign Church Affairs Department, he had taken every measure to prevent the closing of churches and monasteries. In 1960, however, by order of the Council for Russian Orthodox Church Affairs, he was retired, and in December 1961, he died suddenly at the Moscow Botkinsk Hospital under unclear circumstances.[14]

Nun Eufemia recalled this period of the Church's history: "The Glinsk Monastery had not yet been closed when they began driving many of the monks away to who knows where. Once, in Stary Oskol, while Father and I were talking, he dropped his head to the table and began weeping bitterly. Then he asked, 'You wonder why I weep? The Glinsk Hermitage has just been closed!' and he began sobbing again. In the morning his novices came and told us that the Glinsk Hermitage had been closed the day before—as it turned out, at the very moment when Father had been weeping."

Archimandrite Raphael (Karelin), whom the Lord vouchsafed to meet the last Glinsk elders and their novices, recalled,

> The fire of persecutions that blazed throughout the entire country reached the Glinsk Monastery, leaving nothing but its walls intact. The monks, like orphans deprived of their father's home, scattered over hill and dale. The elders foretold that the monastery would open once again, and while living in various regions of the vast country they strove with all their might to ensure that worship according to the Glinsk rule, bequeathed by its godly-wise founder Abbot Philaret, did not cease. They hoped that the time would come when their monastery would once again be opened, and that the wonder-working icon of the Nativity of the Most-Holy Mother of God, would return to its own monastery.[15]

The elders instructed the brethren of the Glinsk Monastery to stand fast on its foundation, so as never to stray from the right path, no matter what life's circumstances, not only not to lose but also to multiply the virtues nurtured there. The brethren were "to hold fast to one another in the world and, when the monastery reopens, to gather once again beneath its arches."[16] Many of the monastic outcasts were received into the bosom of the Iveron land, where the Iveron ascetics, martyrs, and venerable ones made room for the Glinsk monks as fellow brothers. From the Glinsk Monastery of the Nativity of the Most-Holy Mother of God, they went to Iveron,[17] the land allotted to the Mother of God. Always they abode beneath Her protection. The time would come when the Glinsk brethren would again gather together, not on earth but in Heaven"[18]

Throughout his life, Father Ilarion followed the precepts of his elders, often encountering misunderstanding not only from those in authority but also from those for whose salvation he prayed to the point of blood and sweat, laying down his life for them. In undergoing this hard school of true piety and love, grown strong on the foundation of his elders' spiritual experiences, he would look back to his time at the Glinsk Hermitage for guidance in everything. One often heard Father say, "That's how we were taught," or "That's how we did it at the Glinsk Hermitage." Of course, at the same time, he was aware of the spiritual stature of each person within his flock and was indulgent and merciful toward all of them. To many of us, however, in our spiritual sloth and ignorance, this stature sometimes seemed excessive and impracticable, which caused him much suffering.

Father Ilarion took the greatest possible care to maintain the liturgical rule established in the Glinsk Monastery, which included singing, reading, and bowing. The services he conducted were as complete as possible and quite lengthy, particularly the Lenten services. Until his final day at the Bronnitsa church, he always began the Sunday morning services just as they had begun in the Glinsk Hermitage: the Midnight Office, the invariable reading of the akathist to the Mother of God, and on feast days, the All-Night Vigil, the Hours, and so on.

At the Glinsk Hermitage, on the second day of the Feast of the Dormition, the funeral rite (Lamentations) of the Mother of God was served. After the Six Psalms, all in attendance were offered candles. Then, at the end of the service, in deep silence and conscious of the profound reason for what was taking place, the people would process with the tomb around the church three times. This custom was also performed at the Bronnitsa church, but they processed around the church only once. Just as in the Glinsk Hermitage, the priests of Bronnitsa would hold the tomb high aloft, and all those present would pass beneath it; of course, no one in the Bronnitsa church would have lasted through the six- or seven-hour service of the Glinsk Hermitage.

Father Ilarion never received women, who composed the vast majority of the church's visitors, in his cell. In his final years, his novices arranged a small, comfortable reception room at the entrance to the building where he lived, decorated with flowers and lace curtains. In this room, both local worshipers and pilgrims would pour out their hearts to Father, who would be exhausted after the service. Often, they would bring their atheist adult children with the hope that meeting Father would miraculously change their lives, turning them back to God, which often occurred.

Like the Glinsk elders, Father Ilarion considered Christ-like obedience the foundation of spiritual life. He used to say that only by God's grace can one conquer temptations and endure amid spiritual struggle, and that this grace abides only in a humble heart. He grieved greatly for one handmaid of God, who said that the Mother of God and other saints appeared to her. He advised her to pray ardently, to which she insolently responded, "You're just envious." More than once, people observed how disobeying or ignoring Father Ilarion's advice, even in some seemingly insignificant matter, ended in disaster.

In the footsteps of the Glinsk elders, who believed that monks must unfailingly perform the Cell Rule of Five Hundred,[19] Father Ilarion fervently prayed the Jesus Prayer, and suggested to many of his spiritual children that they should pray the Cell Rule of Five Hundred. He warned them, however, not to be willful in this but to adhere to the advice of an experienced mentor. He warned against abstract theorizing about prayers, advising that they be read with childlike simplicity and without any sensual visualization of God and the saints or seeking any particular spiritual sensations.[20] Like the Glinsk elders, he advised consulting the Holy Fathers on various matters, particularly the spiritual mentors of recent times: Holy Hierarchs Ignatius Brianchaninov and Theophan the Recluse (during Father's time at the Glinsk Hermitage, they had not yet been glorified).

Father Ilarion did not approve of earthly attachments to anything or anyone. He particularly warned both monks and laity against the sin of fornication.[21] He guided the souls entrusted him not to himself but to Christ.

In the Bronnitsa churchyard, he established a house of industry, modeled somewhat after the Glinsk house of industry and somewhat reminiscent of the one established in Kronstadt by the Holy Righteous John of Kronstadt, whom he greatly loved and revered. Here, the novices would labor after the service, digging up and fertilizing seedbeds, weeding and watering them, sawing and stacking wood, stacking bricks, sweeping the grounds, and planting flowers. Something was constantly being fixed, painted, or built, such as barns for farming supplies, a well house, and additions to the Sunday school building. Water was carried, trees were pruned, the church walls were whitewashed, and so forth.

He established a mercy society connected to the Sunday school, which generously gave alms to both adults and children, took in orphans, fed the laborers, and maintained the Sunday school. City institutions of all kinds assisted him considerably in this, but the most generous givers of all were the Weghs, Philip and Nadezhda. For fifteen years, they provided charitable aid, and their assistance continued after Philip was assigned to work in St Petersburg. Father Ilarion was eternally grateful to them and prayed for them especially.

Following the example of the work of spiritual enlightenment in Glinsk—including that done at the monastery as well as through the Glinsk leaflets that resumed in 1997 and the Glinsk Theotokian booklets that were constantly published and distributed to pilgrims free of charge—Father Ilarion would compile edifying leaflets, especially before fasts, as well as prefestal leaflets, containing excerpts from the Holy Scriptures, the works of the Holy Fathers, and the lives of great ascetics of God. These leaflets were reprinted and distributed to parishioners in the church and sent to various cities and towns.

The Glinsk Hermitage foreordained many other things in Father Ilarion's life and work. For him, the hermitage always remained the ideal, not only of monastic prosperity but also of the establishment of "a monastery in the world." To the end of his days, he brimmed with reverent love for the monastery and gratitude to its spiritual elders. Had he a choice, he never would have left it.

CHAPTER 3

After the Glinsk Hermitage:
The Elder and the Elders in the World

After leaving the Glinsk Monastery, Father Ilarion was appointed to serve as deacon in the city of Starodub, Orlov Region (now Bryansk Region). Within a few months, Vladyka Leonid (Belgorod Diocese) ordained him a hieromonk and sent him to the village of Borisovka, where the young priest served for about a year. During that year, the church was constantly bursting with the inhabitants of Borisovka and the surrounding area, who came rushing in to fill it. Everyone found room in Father's heart, and he became everyone's familiar and dear friend.

In Borisovka, Father met twenty-year-old Valentina Bondarenko, a nun who immediately became his spiritual daughter and never parted from him thereafter: "Mama was left a widow early on. I was born the year my father was killed in the war. Father Ilarion both fathered and raised me." She served as Father Ilarion's cell attendant to the end of his days.

Before Mother Valentina, his cell attendant had been Mother Anna from the city of Pinsk.[1] As Nun Barbara of the city of Bryansk recalled about Mother Anna, "She was very dedicated to Father. She left her apartment in Pinsk and followed him everywhere. She once told KGB representatives: 'If you give Father a hard time, you'll have me to reckon with...!' 'Lame in one leg, can't work a lick, but when I see Ilarion I come running on the other' was the song Father Ilarion used to sing to Mother Anna. Her last name was Krasovskaya. Father Ilarion was always a merry person, but he lived a very hard life, and was always persecuted by the communists."[2] Always and everywhere, the fiery ministry of God's servant irritated those in authority. "If this cleric spends another year here, he'll make believers of all Borisovka," they fumed. When he left there, Father Ilarion left behind the light of Christ's love, lit by him in the simple hearts of the villagers.

His path next led to the village of Murom, but after a short time, he was reassigned to another village, farther from the city and more isolated. "[B]ut the word of God is not chained."[3] Wherever he was, Father Ilarion's sermons shone with the living, active word of saving truth, and ignited and filled men's hearts with the fire of unquenchable love for God and neighbor.

After the Glinsk Hermitage was closed, his ties with its spiritual mentors were not severed. According to Schema-Archimandrite Elder Vitaly (Vitaly Nikolaevich Sidorenko in the world, 1928–1992), who began his labors in the Glinsk Hermitage in 1948,

> The holy Iveron land received and preserved more than one Russian elder for the world. The first of the Glinsk elders to arrive here was Father Zinovy. After the Glinsk Hermitage was closed for the second time in 1961, Schema-Archimandrite Seraphim moved to Sukhumi, and Schema-Archimandrite Andronik to Tbilisi, along with a number of Glinsk monks (Archimandrite Pimen, Archimandrite Philaret, Hegumen Amvrosy, Hieromonk Nikolai, and others). If one recalls that ancient Iveron was one of the domains of the Mother of God on earth, and that Russia has long been considered the House of the Most-Holy Mother of God, it becomes clear that our Orthodox countries, like spiritual sisters, dwell beneath Her unified Most-pure Protection, and hence our relationship is superior even to that of blood.[4]

Archimandrite Raphael recalled, "The pressures of the Khrushchevian persecutions were felt less strongly in Georgia—the temperament of the Georgian people acted as a kind of buffer. The Georgians and Abkhazians were not the kind to peer into windows to see what their neighbors were up to, and even the authorities treated informers with overt suspicion. The war on religion, or rather the persecution of clergy and believers, was conducted rather unenthusiastically."[5]

The elders cared for their Glinsk children as for their own. "Wherever the monks of the Glinsk monastery happened to be, they knew that they would always have the help and support of Bishop Zinovy. Several of them remained in Georgia for the rest of their lives."[6] Sometimes Father would receive news from them, which always cheered him greatly. Letters from Schema-Archimandrite Elder Andronik and the Monks Veniamin (Selivanov) and Philaret were sent to Father Ilarion.

Still, despite certain laxities on the part of the authorities, Father Raphael noted that "the ideological policing system kept the pressure on from the top."[7] Domestic peace was a long way off. Like other clerics, Father Ilarion was deeply conscious of the tragedy that had happened to monasticism: his brethren flung out of the monastic environment, scattered, dispersed throughout the enormous country, and suffocating in the foreign, worldly atmosphere. Later, after unsuccessful attempts to take up residence at the Trinity-Sergius Lavra and the Pskov Caves Monastery, as his cell attendant Valentina recalled, Father said, "If I had known that I would be unable to remain in a monastery, I would not have become a monk."

Father Ilarion repeatedly traveled to the Caucasus to see Metropolitan Zinovy (Seraphim in the schema) and Elder Andronik (Lukash), who lived in a cottage at the Church of Holy Right-Believing Prince Alexander Nevsky, of which Vladyka Zinovy remained the rector from 1950 until his death. While there, Father Ilarion met with the Glinsk monks Archimandrites Pimen and Philaret, Hegumen Amvrosy, Hieromonk Nikolai, and a novice of Father Andronik, former Glinsk monk Veniamin (Selivanov). When Father Ilarion traveled to Sukhumi, he visited Father Seraphim (Romantsov), who invested all his expertise in spiritually nurturing the hermits,[8] as well as his novice, the Glinsk monk Ieronim, and others.

When Father Andronik reposed in 1974, Hegumen Ilarion[9] moved to Tbilisi. In the cathedral dedicated to Holy Right-Believing Prince Alexander Nevsky, Metropolitan Zinovy and the assembled clergy served the funeral and burial for Schema-Archimandrite Andronik. At the funeral, "former Glinsk Hermitage brother

Hegumen Ilarion (Prikhodko) gave a heartfelt eulogy. In it he emphasized that Fr Andronik was a person of great heart and profound faith, and a ceaseless laborer. His heart was filled with compassionate love for every person; he lived not for himself, but for the people, and well could he be called a "condoler of human souls."[10]

The enactment of the Law on Freedom of Conscience (1990), the collapse of the Communist dictatorship, and the return of brethren to the Glinsk Hermitage in 1994 set the stage for the rebirth of the monastery's traditions of spiritual enlightenment. Articles and books have been written on the lives of many of the Glinsk elders, including a vast composition by Schema-Archimandrite Ioann Maslov on the monastery's nearly five hundred years of work. The Glinsk church calendar was first published in 1997. Publication of the Glinsk leaflets resumed, Glinsk readings were held in various cities (I attended two such readings in Moscow), and video recordings were made on the monastery's history.

From the very first days of the monastery's restoration, the current Glinsk monks came to see Father Ilarion more than once, asking him to accept the office of its superior. However, he chose to remain with those whom he had selflessly served for thirty-four years, having arrived in Bronnitsa on October 18, 1974. He was also preparing for his departure to the mansion of his Heavenly Father. In late May of 2008, His Grace Luka, who was Bishop of Vasilkov and deputy of the Glinsk Hermitage, the hermitage superior Archimandrite Antony, and Archimandrite Sophrony came to accompany Father Ilarion on his final earthly journey.

Even in our sorrowful time of war in the Caucasus, Schema-Archimandrite Vitaly "advised those living in Sukhumi to bring their woes to the grave of Schema-Archimandrite Seraphim (Romantsov), and to tell the elder everything, as though he were alive; or, if it were impossible to go to him, to pray mentally: 'O Lord, through the prayers of my parents and of all who pray for me, help and bless me.'"[11] In this restless, furious time, when it seems the earth itself has shifted and all living things hold their breath in expectation of catastrophic cataclysms, let us also, the spiritual children of our dear Elder Ilarion, tell him of our cares and worries and ask that the Lord might help us and bless us, through the prayers of Father Ilarion, our parents, and all who pray for us.

Father Ilarion himself tirelessly gave thanks throughout his life to the Lord, the Most-Holy Lady Mother of God, his guardian angel, all the saints, and his spiritual mentors of Glinsk, who set him on the right path to God, blessing him for this long spiritual journey and illumining him with grace-imbued rays of unearthly, heavenly love.

CHAPTER 4

The Glinsk Hermitage Today:
The Canonization of Its Elders

At the festivities in honor of the canonization of the Glinsk Elders, Father Ilarion's spiritual children were among those present. They brought back to Veliky Novgorod a holy reliquary containing pieces of the relics of the Glinsk Elders, which was placed in the Protection Cathedral and now brings spiritual consolation to the city's Christians and its many believing guests.

Irina Smirnova of the city of Chudovo wrote her recollections of a pilgrimage she made to the Glinsk Hermitage in her memoirs:

"On May 8, 2008, the Holy Synod of the Ukrainian Orthodox Church, presided over by His Eminence Vladimir, Metropolitan of Kiev and All Ukraine, decreed that the pious ascetics of the nineteenth to twentieth centuries who labored at the Glinsk Hermitage of the Nativity of the Most-Holy Mother of God be numbered with the choir of locally venerated saints. The celebration in honor of their canonization was set for August 16.

"Father Ilarion knew of this joyous event, but was not fated to take part in it. By Father's holy prayers, on August 16 his spiritual children arrived at the Glinsk Hermitage in his stead: Alexei Polikarpov with his son Peter, Galina Baranova, Svetlana Mikhailova, Zoya Nikitina, Ekaterina Dmitrieva, the Drozda and Zhukov couples, and I, the author of these memoirs.

"To travel to the Glinsk Hermitage had always been one of my dearest wishes. For it was there that our dear Father began his monastic journey. And always, whenever talk turned to his life in this monastery, or to its elders, Father's face would shine with an unearthly joy. His cell attendant, Mother Valentina, related how, when the monastery was closed in 1961, Father wept greatly and had no desire whatsoever to abandon it. This is no coincidence, for there it was that he saw true elders, lived with them, and came to understand the art of arts: the salvation of one's soul. His spiritual father was Schema-Archimandrite Andronik, who did much to secure the permission of the Soviet authorities to accept Father as a brother of the Glinsk Hermitage, and always treated Father Ilarion with maternal care and love. All his life Father pined for his native monastery, and in his church in Bronnitsa he conducted the divine services according to the Glinsk schedule: Divine Liturgy always began at nine o'clock, preceded by the reading of the Psalter and akathists, and the All-Night Vigil began at four o'clock in the evening.

"In addition to prayer in church, there in the monastery Father tasted the sweetness of the Jesus Prayer. Truly, the Glinsk Hermitage was a spiritual cradle for our Father. Hence, when the monastery dean, Archimandrite Antony, invited Father Ilarion's spiritual children to take part in the festivities in honor of the Glinsk Elders' canonization, many received this invitation with great joy.

"We traveled there by train, first to Moscow, then to the Tereshchenko station, where we were met by car and driven to the Glinsk Hermitage.

"We arrived several days before the upcoming festivities, so we tried to help the monastery brethren as much as we could to prepare to receive the many anticipated pilgrims. In spite of our obediences, during our breaks we were able to visit the place of the appearance of the wonder-working icon of the Nativity of the Mother of God, where in 2002 a chapel had been built and consecrated. Before, there had been a neighboring skete here, beside which the monastery cemetery was located. By our time, however, very little remained of it. At the cemetery, in the course of preparing for the canonization of the monastery brethren, using archival documents and the memoirs of former brethren of the monastery, archeologists located several of the elders' graves, in particular the highly venerated grave of Elder Theodotus (Levchenko).

"From the monastery brethren we likewise learned of the finding of the relics of Elder Ioannicius (Gomolko), which clearly testifies to God's help in finding the relics of the Glinsk Elders. From the *Glinsk Paterikon* we know that, while serving as superior of the Glinsk Hermitage in the early twentieth century, Father Ioanniky was unjustly persecuted, leading to his departure from the monastery. As he was leaving, a miracle occurred: the elder walked across the flooded meadow as though it were dry land. This miracle, which occurred before the very eyes of the monastery brethren, proved his innocence. From that time on, none of the brethren ever saw Father Ioanniky again, and nothing was known about his life thereafter.

"Not without God's providence, while in Russia Archimandrite Antony, the current dean of the hermitage, learned from a certain handmaid of God that on the outskirts of the city of Rylsk, in the Kursk Region, a monk of the Glinsk Hermitage was buried—Schema-Archimandrite Ioanniky. A comparison of details from this monk's life with archival data and service records lead to the conclusion that this was indeed the very same Father Ioanniky. It came to light that he had lived out the last years of his life in Russia in seclusion, in the home of a pious family. When the materials for the elder's canonization were submitted for consideration to the Holy Synod of the Ukrainian Orthodox Church, his relics were miraculously found.

"We likewise visited the site of the far skete, where there is a blessed stream, and several small houses inhabited by former brethren of the monastery who have left it voluntarily.

"Practically nothing is left of the Glinsk Hermitage from Father Ilarion's time there. The Church of the Exaltation of the Cross had been razed not long before our arrival, and we walked to the site not far from the monastery where the ancient, mighty timbers, boards, and plasterwork had been dumped into a pile—all that had once been the hospital building with the Church of the Exaltation of the Cross. We walked among them and broke off several small pieces as keepsakes—after all, they had been sanctified by the prayers of more than one generation of Glinsk monks, including our own dear in the Lord Father Ilarion.

"During our stay at the monastery we tried to attend all the divine services served at St Nicholas Church, consecrated in 2001. It contains the chief holy things of the Glinsk Hermitage. In the right side chapel we venerated the relics of the monastery superior, Schema-Archimandrite Seraphim (Amelin). They were first found in 1961, during the relocation of the reposed elders from the church to the common brothers' cemetery. All the brethren had been struck by the fact that the elder's vestments and coffin were untouched by decay.

"In addition, the church houses the Glinsk Wonder-Working Image of the Savior Not-Made-By-Human-Hands. It was found anew in July of 2006, and our own Father Ilarion was instrumental in returning this beloved holy icon to the monastery.

"In the summer of 2006 the monastery brethren called Father Ilarion in Bronnitsa and told him that a certain handmaid of God had in her possession the wonder-working Glinsk icon of the Savior, but that she was unwilling to return it to the monastery. Father Ilarion then wrote her a letter, a copy of which has survived in the papers Father left behind. In this letter, dated June 26, 2006, Archimandrite Ilarion wrote the following:

"'I have learned that you have in your care the Image of the Savior Not-Made-By-Human-Hands which was previously located in the Glinsk Hermitage of the Nativity of the Most-Holy Mother of God. It stood in an icon case on the right-hand side, near the Kliros. Each Sunday morning we would sing an akathist before it.

"'If you have this icon, you must absolutely give it back to the monastery. This holy icon's place is in the Holy Monastery. I ask you sincerely to do this, bowing down at your feet. I would come myself, if I had the strength....'

"The holy icon soon returned to its monastery.

"Beside this wonder-working image, on a small analogion, stood an ark with relics of the holy God-pleasers, given to the Glinsk Hermitage by Father Ilarion not long before his death. He was very glad to learn that his beloved monastery had begun to actively revive, and gave it many of his personal effects (priestly vestments, books, icons) before his repose.

"Aside from St Nicholas Church, the monastery has yet another barbican church dedicated to the Iveron Icon of the Mother of God, consecrated in 1999. Prior to their glorification, the relics of the eight Glinsk Elders were located in the altar. All his life Father Ilarion greatly venerated the Iveron Icon of the Mother of God. In the Bronnitsa church the Iveron icon hung on the lowest tier of the iconostas. Upon entering the altar, Father would always venerate it reverently, and in his sermons on the icon's feast he would always mention the Glinsk Monastery, where the wonder-working Iveron Icon of the Most-Holy Mother of God was kept until the monastery was first closed by the Soviet authorities. Clearly, it was through Father's prayers, and for the sake of his love for this icon, that we were able to spend all night in the Iveron church, where holy items in little bags were laid out to be given in blessing to the many pilgrims expected. Archimandrite Antony brought the relics out of the altar, and we venerated them.

"Finally, unobtrusively, August 16 arrived. On the eve, at the All-Night Vigil, the service to Venerable Anthony the Roman was sung and read. It was a joy to have the commemoration of our Novgorodian saint coincide with the festivities for the Glinsk Elders' glorification. On the actual day of the glorification, two Divine Liturgies were served. The early liturgy was served in the Iveron church, at which we communed with Archimandrite Antony's blessing. Later, the Divine Liturgy was served in the yard in front of the brother's refectory. A temporary altar was erected, before which was placed the reliquary containing the relics of the Glinsk ascetics. At one time the Nativity of the Mother of God Cathedral had stood on this site. His Eminence Vladimir, Metropolitan of Kiev and all Ukraine and Archimandrite of the Glinsk Hermitage, presided at the service. A great many archbishops, bishops, and priests concelebrated with Vladyka.

"During the Divine Service a statement from the minute book of the Holy Synod of the Ukrainian Orthodox Church was read, containing the resolution that the thirteen Glinsk Elders be glorified as locally venerated saints, along with short accounts of the lives of the Glinsk ascetics: Hegumen Philaret (Danilevsky);

Schema-Archimandrites Iliodor (Golovanitsky), Ioannicius (Gomolko), and Seraphim (Amelin); Archimandrite Innocent (Stepanov); Hieroschemamonks Basil (Kishkin) and Macarius (Sharov); Schemamonks Luke (Shvets), Archippus (Shestakov), and Euphemius (Lyubimchenko); and Monks Theodotus (Levchenko), Martyrius (Kirichenko), and Dositheus (Kolchenkov). To the singing of the troparion to the Glinsk saints, Archimandrites Sophrony and Antony came out of the altar carrying the icon of the Synaxis of the Venerable Fathers of Glinsk. Metropolitan Vladimir, primate of the Ukrainian Orthodox Church, prayerfully venerated the icon and the holy relics of the newly glorified saints for the first time. He then sincerely congratulated all present with this momentous occasion in the life of the Church. That day several thousand people communed at the Divine Liturgy. Despite the oppressive heat and the press of the crowd, on that festive day we felt light-hearted and joyous.

"The people did not disperse for some time after the service. Some ate at the tables set up right in the yard in front of St Nicholas Church; others tried to venerate the holy relics of the Glinsk Elders once more in parting. Of the thirteen newly-glorified saints, the relics of only nine were found. Eight of these (the venerable Philaret, Innocent, Ioannicius, Iliodor, Seraphim, Macarius, Archippus, and Theodotus) rest in the Glinsk Hermitage; the relics of Venerable Basil were found in the Ploshchansk Monastery of the Bryansk diocese.

"In the evening the reliquaries were moved to St Nicholas Church, and all who were present at the Divine Liturgy the next day felt the particular prayerful proximity of these holy God-pleasers.

"During these days at the Glinsk Hermitage, I constantly caught myself thinking how much it reminded me of Optina—the same pines, the same extraordinary, penetrating silence, the same prayerful aura. As if in confirmation of my thoughts I suddenly saw Schema-Hegumen Iliya, who had come from the Optina Hermitage for the celebration, walking about the monastery. Gazing at this elder and man of prayer, I involuntarily thought how badly the modern Glinsk Hermitage, under reconstruction, was in want of experienced spiritual mentors such as he.

"As I took my leave of this holy monastery which had become so dear to my heart, I left it with the prayerful wish that it might see the restoration of Glinsk eldership, about which not a few wonderful books have already been written, and with which, thanks to our spiritual father Archimandrite Ilarion and by God's mercy, we had been vouchsafed some little contact."

CHAPTER 5

His Spiritual Father, Ioann (Krestyankin), and Other Mentors

When the Glinsk elders were no more, over the course of several years, Father Ilarion visited Father Archimandrite Seraphim (Tyapochkin, 1894–1982)[1] in the village of Rakitnoye, Belgorod Region, where the elder served at St Nicholas Church from 1961 until his death. It was Schema-Archimandrite Andronik (Lukash) who blessed Father Dimitry to take the monastic tonsure with the name Seraphim. This sheds some light on the question of what led Hieromonk Ilarion to Elder Seraphim: Schema-Archimandrites Andronik and Seraphim (Romantsov) were the spiritual guides of Father Seraphim (Tyapochkin). Those who were vouchsafed to resort to the aid of this great ascetic, following his instructions and confessing to him, wrote of him with a sense of profound, heartfelt reverence and tenderness: "He radiated the light of righteousness."[2]

The memory of this amazing elder filled Father Ilarion's heart with love for him, strengthening in Father the spirit of Christian love for his flock and giving him strength in his labors on behalf of the suffering. It helped him to bear his own sorrows and comfort others in sorrow at difficult times in their lives. Father Seraphim and Father Ilarion loved and respected each other very much, and each took seriously the opinion of his questioner.

Father Ilarion's meeting with Father Ioann (Krestyankin) left an indelible impression on his heart. With profound reverence, Father Ilarion described in a sermon his first meeting with Father Ioann at the holy Glinsk Hermitage in 1957, which roused feelings of profound love for his future spiritual father and of profound devotion to him. In a short sketch dedicated to the life and work of Father Ioann in gratitude for his spiritual guidance, and in honor of the elder's ninety-fourth birthday, Father Ilarion recalled, "I was a novice monk, awash with pride and vainglory, and in you I saw a wise, experienced elder, full of selfless love, humility, and meekness. This meeting left in my soul a sincere and most profound respect and love for you, and a sense of profound devotion to you."

They would later meet several times briefly in the Trinity-Sergius Lavra and the Pskov Caves Monastery. Father Ilarion became better acquainted with Father Ioann in 1967, when the latter came to live at the Dormition Caves Monastery. "It was then," recalled Father Ilarion, "that, without the slightest wavering, I chose you, as a wise elder, to be my spiritual mentor, though at the time I told you nothing of this."

Subsequently, during his studies at the Leningrad Theological Academy, Father Ilarion would travel to the monastery several times a year. He lived there for a time, guided by the wise advice and instruction of Father Ioann: "You became the person closest to me, an irreplaceable and beloved father ... a wise, multifaceted spiritual mentor, a good shepherd who, in accordance with Christ's words, *laid down his life for the sheep*."

The young hieromonk had a constant desire to study, his mind and heart aspiring toward a deeper knowledge of the truth of Divine Scripture. The elders blessed him to study in Zagorsk (now Sergiev Posad). After successfully passing his entrance exams, he entered the Moscow Theological Seminary. Within three months, he was expelled for having no registration of domicile. His first year of studies was very difficult, as he had not been enrolled in a school for many years. Yet, his thirst for knowledge and determination to overcome the difficulties gained the upper hand, and in the years of study that followed at the seminary and the Leningrad Theological Academy, Father Ilarion was primarily an "A" student.

Father was then obliged to travel to Pechory in hopes of becoming a clergyman at the Pskov Caves Monastery. Hierodeacon Nikon

(Murzatov) of the St Petersburg Monastery of Saint John recalled Father Ilarion during this period:

> I have known Fr Ilarion since 1963, when he lived at the Pskov Caves Monastery and served his obedience there, serving and singing in the choir. I also went to the monastery to sing in the mixed brothers' choir, lead by Hieromonk Innokenty. We owned a cottage in Pechory, and I lived there, going to the monastery to serve my obediences. In those years I had more personal contact with Archimandrite Agafangel, who had come from Jerusalem.
>
> Fr Ilarion, with his athletic stature, impressed me by the power of his voice, but not just by its power. In his voice one sensed a firm faith, a boldness before the Savior and His Most-pure Mother, composure, purposefulness, and the penitential wail of the soul. He read canons and akathists beautifully, praying articulately and unhurriedly from the very depths of his soul. He was truly an adornment for the Pskov Caves Monastery. All the congregation loved him: people would always run to him for his blessing and advice, and he would always answer them with love, sometimes responding with good-natured humor, though at other times he could be strict with certain individuals. That is how I remembered him from my frequent requests for his blessing. Later, he and I corresponded. I greeted him with the feasts of Christ's Nativity and Holy Pascha on behalf of my brother Archimandrite Germogen, and he always answered us in detail. We two brethren were kindred spirits. When he fell seriously ill he wrote a letter asking for our holy prayers, and he always sent us presents of expensive foods.
>
> We always keep our dear Father in prayerful remembrance.

Father Ilarion could not long remain a brother of the Pskov Caves Monastery without a registration of domicile, and he left for Leningrad. While there, he was finally registered, and he entered the Leningrad Theological Seminary.

CHAPTER 6

The Leningrad Years

Whilst studying at the Leningrad Theological Seminary, Father Ilarion also served as the Dean of the Seminary church. Archbishop Prokl of Ulyanovsk and Melekessk,[1] who lives in the city of Ulyanovsk, recounted this time, saying: "Father Ilarion was a model of piety. He treated the students extremely well. He was lenient with all, and enjoyed the people's love and respect. This was a deeply profound, prayerfully minded person. He loved to serve and sing at early Liturgy. Father loved to pray, and read the scriptural lessons himself. At meals he sat at the head of the monastic table."

Mother Galina of Veliky Novgorod had similar words of praise: "During Father Valentin's studies at the Theological Seminary, Father Ilarion was serving there as dean. The professors and students treated him with great respect. He was strict and quite demanding, but he always tried to correct people by instructing, never by demeaning them. He was excellently versed in the church typicon, and maintained order in the church."

After graduating from the Seminary, Father entered the Leningrad Theological Academy in 1967 to further his theological education. In all, his studies continued for around ten years. In the Academy, he listened to his Orthodox professors. Of these, his best-loved professor and the one who made the greatest impression on him was Professor Nikolai Dimitrievich Uspensky, who was born in the Novgorod Region, the son of a priest. Father Ilarion remained deeply grateful to all of the professors of the Theological Seminary and the Academy throughout his life, and frequently recalled them as being very humble and well educated, but it was Professor Nikolai Dimitrievich Uspensky who he remembered with particular warmth and love. Archpriest Vladimir Sorokin[2] likewise spoke of him with great fondness: "This was our famous, universally revered professor, doctor, and liturgist."

In an interview conducted by Irina Vladimirovna Smirnova regarding the Seminary and Academy professors at the time of Father Ilarion's studies there, Father Vladimir (Sorokin) said,

> I will give you a small book that lists all the professors that taught Fr Ilarion. After some thought about how best to provide an illustrative definition of "succession" with regard to theological education, and to give a better sense of the generational connection, I drew three pictures that now hang in the senior common room of the Saint Petersburg Orthodox Theological Academy. One depicts the rectors who have reposed, another depicts the pre-revolutionary professors and lecturers, and the third depicts the post-revolutionary faculty—those who resurrected the theological schools after 1945. Some time later the idea matured of creating a fourth picture, representing the keepers and confessors of the faith of the twentieth century, persecuted, mocked, of whom the whole world was not worthy.

We opened the book Father Vladimir had given us and read the following: "The result was a historical series under the common title of 'Succession,' with sections on 'The Guardians,' 'Theology and Life,' 'Troubled Years: A Time of Trial,' and 'From Nonexistence to Nonexistence.' All told, the four pictures depict one hundred and seventy two persons."[3] We then read on:

> In a city on the Neva, the third period in the history of theological education—"From Nonexistence to Being"—began the year that World War II ended. It began inauspiciously, with the organization of theological and pastoral courses in the fall of 1945.... Within just one year, on October 14, 1946, the Leningrad Theological Academy and Seminary were opened on the base of the theological courses.... Within a few years the best graduates of the resurrected

Theological School began serving ecclesiastical obediences of considerable responsibility, becoming bishops, rectors of large parishes, and officials at Synodal establishments.[4]

Father Vladimir pointed out some of the academy professors of Father Ilarion's time in a photograph accompanied by their biographies. He then elaborated on his memories of Father Ilarion:

"I remember Father Ilarion from the time of his studies at the Theological Academy. At the time I was already a lecturer, board secretary, and priest, and I remember him quite well in connection with the Divine Services: he had a deep reverence for the church typicon. He had a good voice and sang very well, always leading the singing of the clergy, and was remarkably zealous in the Divine Services. He was the dean of our church, and he would always have everything clearly and precisely prepared ahead of time, making sure everyone was in his place. It should be borne in mind that the seminary and academy churches were educational churches. Metropolitan Nikodim was at the Academy at the time, and he was very active in ordaining students. Hence, the students had to be taught, and it was the dean's task to assist them to stand properly, and to cross themselves properly, and to hold their service books properly, and to perform the service reverently. All of these things are of great importance, but young people are often absent-minded and distracted. Considerable time goes by before a young man 'gets into' or 'grows into' the service. But Father Ilarion patiently corrected and taught each one of them, helping everyone and enjoying considerable authority among the students—all the more so because he had come to the Academy already as a hieromonk, and a monk from an excellent monastery, at that. He did not advertise or flaunt the fact, however; his behavior was perfectly proper.

"Metropolitan Nikodim appreciated Father Ilarion very much, and valued him highly. After he completed his studies, his superiors wanted to retain him at the Academy as a professorial scholar, in the capacity of lecturer. Nothing came of this, however: this was still the era of Soviet power. Our commissioner at the time was Egor Semenovich Zharinov, who kept a watchful eye on the Academy to ensure that it did not look too presentable. His task was to remove as many authoritative clergymen from the students' environment as possible. Metropolitan Nikodim worked hard to defend Father Ilarion, supporting him in every way and trying to clear a path for him: he wanted very much to retain him for the Academy. In the latter he failed, but he did manage to have Father Ilarion transferred to service in Novgorod. People like Father Ilarion, Father Philaret, and several other young monks were the core of the Academy. They were, in a way, its spiritual elite. Their deportment was most respectable, and they adhered strictly to the rules, so that no accusation could be made against them at any level.

"Let's face it—we had all kinds of young monks that Vladyka Nikodim tonsured. Many of them caused considerable hassles and created problems. Well do I remember the complicated situation at the time: the authorities controlled everything, harassing everyone, and at the same time there were plenty of internal problems. On top of everything, a dissident movement was gaining momentum among people who, on the one hand, were dissatisfied with the Soviet government, and on the other, were trying to express this through the church structure, luring young seminarians and monks into their ranks. This was a very serious problem, and one not easily solved, and fathers such as Ilarion, Philaret, and others proved themselves Orthodox rocks of faith. They could not be reproached in any respect—either for their studies, or discipline, or morals, or their civil stance. If they had to vote, they went and voted; if they had to support a community land improvement project, they were glad to oblige; say 'sing,' and they sang. All their obediences they performed without a murmur and with considerable skill. I was part of the Academy administration, and the dean of the church, assistant, or board secretary are what one might call unskilled laborers. After all, as with anything, someone has to keep things clean and in order, make sure that the icons are hung straight, see to it that the students behave themselves properly, and the like. We were all members of a single, close-knit team.

"Metropolitan Nikodim was both very strict and very busy. The greater part of his time he spent in Moscow, but when he came here he immediately went to the church, and if he found a single breach of order we would be in considerable trouble. This kept things highly disciplined: the hall was always in festive array, and everyone was always on his toes, especially during Great Lent, when Vladyka Nikodim would come to us during the First Week for the reading of the Great Canon of Saint Andrew of Crete. He always stood below the kliros, and made prostrations with such vigor (along with Father Ilarion in the altar) that one would think: so that's what monks are like—that's how to make prostrations and pray.

"Vladyka Nikodim frequently tonsured, and in this Father Ilarion was his indispensable helper. He really and truly loved the services, loved the Church, and loved to do good to people in every way, particularly by way of suggestions to ensure that everything was as it should be. There are people who are more or less pious, humble, and modest, but passively. Father Ilarion, on the contrary, was all of the above, but quite actively so. He rushed to do good, prompting, correcting, striving to ensure that everything was at the very highest level. Being a very kind and humble person, he would do whatever it took to correct something done incorrectly, and would succeed without fail in awakening in a person the need to serve responsibly, beautifully, and with dignity. This cannot be taken away from Father Ilarion. He epitomized monasticism in its very worthiest light. I always remember him with deep gratitude. So much time has passed, and now you really understand (I still teach at the Theological Academy and Seminary) how important it is that, from the moment of ordination, a person become accustomed to a definite norm, a definite standard of interaction with the world around him, a definite standard in his relationships with people. If he becomes accustomed to singing beautifully, he will sing beautifully. If he becomes accustomed to caring for his neighbor, he will care for him always. This is very important, and Father Ilarion had this within him.

"Later, after he ended up in Novgorod under Vladyka Antony, I often travelled there, and Father Ilarion and I met as the best of friends and recalled times past. He was a godly man, of course. The Church at the time was, unquestionably, in an unusual position.

Some say, and write, that it was imprisoned—by communism, by ideology, etc. But you know, when you looked at Father Ilarion, and when you remember him now, you had and have no sense that he was in any prison, under anyone's Damocles' sword. He always behaved in such a way that no one and no authority could accuse him of anything. To be sure, the government had no desire for such people to be visible: they tried to weed them out, driving them off into no-man's land on various pretexts.

"Father Ilarion's registration of domicile expired, and in Soviet times this was of pivotal importance: if your registration expired, they would take advantage of the situation and refuse to renew it, and you were doomed to a tortuous ordeal. It was all very simple: if a person has no registration of domicile, we are not allowed to house him in the dormitory; if we don't discharge him from the dormitory, we won't be allowed to register the next person there. We were forced to discharge Father Ilarion, and he was transferred to service in Novgorod. And yet, in the history of theological education, and in the history of the Russian Church, his service to God and men is one of the best pages in the history of the Church in the twentieth century.

"There was no vanity in him, no vainglory; he was not a combative person. If something was wrong, he would explain by a joke or a hint how a person ought to behave, or he would say: 'Don't pester me.' And that was it, on any issue—end of discussion.

"He wrote a most important thesis on the Holy Hierarch Basil the Great, based on the Holy Fathers. For that time, this was highly significant since, I repeat, the time was an extraordinary one. The sacrament of repentance is the sacrament where a person confesses before the Lord, of course, but nevertheless establishes a certain inner spiritual contact with the person confessing him. And many people confessed to Father Ilarion. He was a good spiritual father.

"I cannot say that he had many followers of the hysterical persuasion, so to speak. He did not like hysterics—these hysterical women who are always gasping and exclaiming, running around in their headscarves, fussing and getting excited. His was a moderate public. The intelligentsia at the time was constantly vacillating in its choice of path, but Father Ilarion walked the royal path, confessing everyone precisely, evenly, and clearly. The students always came to him on Friday of the First Week of Great Lent and on Great Thursday of Holy Week, as well as all day on Wednesday after the Presanctified Liturgy. On these days, when the Academy truly lives this sacrament, Father Ilarion and a few other monks would confess all of us—lecturers, students, and staff. This custom stands to this day.

"Yes, Father Ilarion was a very, very worthy person, and a person of much grace. I am very grateful to him, and above all I am grateful to the Lord that, at a time when the Academy was in a very complicated position, He sent people like this (Vladyka Nikodim and Father Ilarion) who succeeded in keeping the situation in hand, and the Academy was not closed then, but was preserved.

"I met with Father Ilarion later, when he was already an Archimandrite and an elder revered in the Novgorod Diocese. Remarkably, he was just as I remember him: open, a little naive, direct, and spiritually at ease. One sensed that he had nothing to hide and no one to hide from—he never had ulterior motives. If he thought someone needed a lecture, he lectured openly, without any ambiguity. 'Let's have no more such foolishness,' he would say. 'Take care. Off you go.' Arguing with him was impossible: either do as you ought in the Church, or else don't play the fool—leave. He was a monk who did not amass mentally ill people and eldresses about him in a strange sort of brother-and-sisterhood. It was no accident, once again, that he wrote a work on repentance, for in repentance what is particularly important?—sobriety, common sense, and sound reasoning (according to the Apostle Paul). He emphasized that confession must be an inner state, so as to avoid a contradiction between reason and conscience, between a person's words and his actions and life. Repentance raises a person up to the level of his relationship with the Lord in love, in faith, and in hope, rather than a person constantly feeling himself burdened by sin.

"Father Ilarion's work is very indicative. This was very much his subject, since he could see and understand a person. We had foreigners studying there at the time—Ethiopians from Africa.

Vladyka Nikodim opened the doors to them to keep the Academy from being closed (this was one way of doing so). One might think that strict monks would have said, 'What do we need foreigners here for?' (Just as some say today, 'There he goes, spending time with foreigners again….') But they came to the church, prayed with us, ate with us in the refectory—they were our students. What were we to do? Shun them? Persecute them? Nothing of the sort. Father Ilarion gave them a place to pray, and a place to sing hymns, and this was not a problem; this was not considered a betrayal of Orthodoxy. We never relinquished our own Orthodox ways, however, and none of them ever entered the altar. This was the Ethiopian church, after all, and they have their own calendar, their own peculiarities. Father Ilarion understood clearly and precisely that our people in no way suffered from this, but on the contrary had the opportunity to watch and listen. They lived with us, and took an interest in everything.

"Father Ilarion's view was very calm and confident because he knew his Orthodoxy extremely well—its services, its catechism, and its tradition. It has been proven that if a person knows well what is his own, he defends it, and he then finds it easy to compare what is his own to what is foreign. When a person does not know what is his own, or knows it poorly, or doubts it, he is constantly afraid that someone may lure or divert him from the right path, and he is afraid even to make comparisons. He who fears to compare is he who truly does not know what is his own.

"Father Ilarion had one overwhelming trait: he knew what was his own. He was not afraid to enter into dialogue with anyone, since he knew well what was his own. This was power, and this was of great value in him. This is why they wished to retain him at the Academy, but the times were against him. Nevertheless, he remained in the Church, and was assigned to the Novgorod Diocese.

"He was truly a good person. I recall him with deep gratitude, and I set him as an example for my students. 'If a person—monk, priest, or layman—knows that which is his own,' I tell them, 'he will have fewer doubts and fears.' 'They're lining their bellies at our expense!' 'They've sold us out!' 'We've betrayed Orthodoxy!' etc. How can you betray Orthodoxy? Here's a simple example: is it really possible to somehow change the Divine Liturgy? No, it's not. No one will support it! And if the priest goes and says: 'Let's serve the Divine Liturgy without the Cherubic Hymn,' the people will promptly say: 'No, Father, that's not how we do it here.' And what's the priest going to do? Why, no such priest could exist, so much is this the natural established order in the Church.

"It should be emphasized again and again that Father Ilarion treated very seriously the work entrusted him by God: he had a very highly developed sense of responsibility. Yes, he talked with the Ethiopians, comparing what was his with what was theirs, and vice versa (the authorities took this as a sign of nonaggression and loyalty on our part). But he didn't say to them: 'Serve our Liturgy.' Such a thing would be unthinkable, just like the things one hears today: 'Did you hear? Our Patriarch met with so-and-so and so-and-so.' Vladyka Nikodim was faulted by some for his meetings with people of various confessions. Yet these people 'held on' to Orthodoxy, and through such meetings and conversations came to better know, and more highly value what was their own. Thanks to them, the communists left us, the Orthodox Church, alone.

"Father Ilarion was one of those who retained the Orthodox faith, Orthodox traditions, and Orthodox service orders, thereby making it possible for Russia to stand fast on this firm cornerstone. In this lies the contribution of Father Ilarion and the other monks for the Church in the twentieth century. They truly helped the Church to endure and survive. The Church herself is invincible, and the gates of hell shall not prevail against her, but they tried to obliterate the people…!

"I always, always remember Father Ilarion with deep gratitude. May the Lord grant him the heavenly kingdom."

After defending his candidate's thesis, "New Testament and Patristic Teaching on the Sacrament of Repentance,"[5] mentored by Professor Archpriest L. Voronov, Father Ilarion graduated the Academy with honors and was offered a position there as a lecturer. This proved impossible, however, since Father's proof of residence was unregistered; that is, he refused to serve in the KGB. They wanted to send him to some out-of-the-way corner, such as Vnutovo or someplace even farther away, but God was merciful. It was no coincidence that Mother Anna had a dream from which she concluded, "They're not going to drive you away."

For a time, Father Ilarion remained at the Academy. As Galina Aleksandrovna Zhuravleva of the city of Severodvinsk recalled, "In late May of 1967 I came to Leningrad and attended several lectures by Fr Ilarion at the Academy. He had a small cell there, where he both lived and held conversations with his visitors, of whom there were many." In the summer of 1972, Father Ilarion was accepted as one of the brethren of Trinity-Sergius Lavra. Here also, however, the current law was triggered, according to which he could not remain in the lavra without registration of domicile.

After many ordeals, about which he never murmured (calling to mind the Gospel instruction, "[A]ll who desire to live godly in Christ Jesus will suffer persecution"[6]), the priest Ilarion Prikhodko remained in the Novgorod Diocese, where he had been sent by Metropolitan Nikodim, and was assigned to serve at the Church of the Holy Apostle Philip. Father Ilarion arrived in Novgorod on July 28, 1973.

CHAPTER 7

At the Church of the Holy Apostle Philip in Novgorod

In the same year, 1973, Father Ilarion was elevated to the rank of Hegumen. The Glinsk elders immediately responded to this spiritual occasion:

Truly Christ is Risen!

Beloved Fr Hegumen Ilarion!

In these joyous days we congratulate you with your hegumenship, and wish you continued spiritual prosperity.

We are glad to hear that men from among the Glinsk brethren are elevated as they merit, and yet solely for their humility.

May God bless you for the gifts you sent!

We received them on time and in their entirety.

Grandfather is still sick, and is flat on his back. He eats and talks very little. Grandfather apparently lives by the prayers of the Russian empire. He recently had a major stroke. We thought he would leave us, but so far, thank God, we have spent Pascha together.

Fr Isidore likewise was made a Hegumen on Pascha.

Fr Iliya Barakovsky died on Lazarus Saturday.

Again, may God bless you for your thoughtfulness and news.

We wish you every blessing and mercy from the Risen Savior.

Your friends and family

Dcn. Andronik

M. Veniamin

A. Philaret

P.S. Please give eternal, living paschal greetings from all of us to Hegumen Makary, Fr Ioann, and Fr Nektary.

Father began his ecclesiastical service at a difficult period for the Russian Orthodox Church. It was a time when the Church was once again subjected to the attacks of the Soviet authorities, with new repressions and administrative abuses. All of Russia's surviving churches were turned into utility facilities. "Everything was forbidden, except by special permission from the Central Committee."[1] The godless authorities interpreted any initiative as an attempt at resistance. The atmosphere in Novgorod Region at the time may be judged, among other things, by the following type of documents:

> Certificate: Issued in confirmation that the Trubichinsk Village Soviet (Novgorod Region) has no objection to a priest attending the deceased (full name) in the village of Ustie. April 10, 1961.[2]

> Request: To St Nicholas Cathedral, city of Novgorod. We request that a priest come to our apartment to visit the ailing (full name) to perform a religious rite. The inhabitants of our apartment block do not object to visits from church clerics. Here are their signatures ... 07.27.1961.[3]

Regarding the church services of Vladyka Nikodim (Rotov), the commissioner for Novgorod Region wrote in his report that "everything that takes place in the church is intended to drive believers to distraction—to rouse them to adoration bordering on hallucination."[4] After his meetings with the commissioner for religious affairs, Vladyka Nikodim sometimes felt as though he had been talking to a brick wall. Of course, Father Ilarion likewise experienced this wall during his time in Novgorod, and even his ardent disposition could not topple it. He became a thorn in the side of the local authorities. For the faithful, however—not only the parishoners of Church of the Holy Apostle Philip, but also all the faithful of Novgorod and the region—he proved a true spiritual treasure. In his sermons, he spoke on the meaning of spiritual life, what it means to cleanse one's heart, how the ascetics attained true knowledge of God, the sweet joy of life in God and for God and neighbor, the significance of reading the word of God, and the necessity of prayer, humility, patience, and the other virtues in the life of a Christian.

His sermons always began and ended with a call to repentance for having departed from God and for living a godless way of life. They sounded like a confession of his life in Christ. He gave his sermons with internal power and faith, as though he were speaking of something that had just now happened to him. Their grace-imbued power was instantly communicated to his listeners, penetrating deeply into their hearts. Crowds of people came to listen to this new pastor and confess to him. All were struck by his noble strictness and courage. According to Anna Mikhailovna Gorlova, a parishioner,

> I recall how we would confess to Father the first year he spent in Novgorod. It was truly a shock—not only for us, but for him as well. Up until then, no one had asked whether we had prepared for confession, or fasted. And all of a sudden Fr Ilarion was asking each of us in detail. It was during the Dormition Fast, in the lower temple at St Philip Church. We stood there, shaking, before him. Father had his head in his hands (he liked to give us a full-scale view of our sins): "How can this be?! What on earth is this?! How can you do that?!" Soon, however, his inquisitions gave way to compassion and admonition. We were afraid of him, but at the same time we could no longer imagine our spiritual life without him. And when he was transferred to Bronnitsa, people trickled there after him.

"Archimandrite Fr Ilarion—what a great name, and with a life to match," recalled Priest Victor (Petirnev). "His patron saint was Saint Ilarion the Great. And when the day of Venerable Ilarion the

Great approaches, one immediately sees Archimandrite Fr Ilarion, a living example of greatness.

"When I first saw Fr Ilarion on Novgorodian soil in the early 1970s, I was delighted with his outward appearance: he was a tall man with handsome facial features, and handsome in every way. But what struck me was his voice. His voice knew no bounds. He would fly to the heavens and return to earth, so that we could pray. With his powerful voice he reminded us where we were, and by his prayer and his energy he attuned us to pray. I myself, being a deacon at St Philip Church where we served together, learned from him how to serve. His powerful, melodic voice gladdened me, and I felt glad that we had such a wonderful priest. Sadly, today there is no such voice in our diocese.

"One had to be at Fr Ilarion's services to understand him. By his serving he raised us up on high, to God. And when the Liturgy ended he would give a wonderful sermon. In those years I never heard anyone give such sermons. Such intellect, such character, such power of argument they held! And when he had finished his sermon, the church would be quiet. All one would hear was the sound of his voice reverberating in the cupola.

"It is a great pity that Fr Ilarion spent so little time in Novgorod. He was transferred to the village of Bronnitsa. I did not lose touch with him, however, since the Bronnitsa church is the church of my childhood and youth, where I received my spiritual upbringing.

"Fr Ilarion and I often spoke on things both spiritual and personal. I was amazed by his intellect, wisdom, and sense of friendliness. And I was always surprised at how Fr Ilarion would address me using the formal 'you.' When he became the spiritual father for all of us clergymen, many priests would travel to him for advice. And in his quiet, mild, warm voice he would attune us to the spiritual life.

"Archimandrite Fr Ilarion will always be a model for me in life. From him I learned service, diligence, the typicon of the Holy Church, and how to deal with people. He did not spare himself. Service to God and men—this was his purpose in life. And the Lord was always with him. He lived a long and necessary life, and left behind many who remember and pray for him. We believe that he remembers and prays for us, as well."[5]

The patience of the city authorities was finally exhausted. The new priest was summoned, reprimanded, and berated for his "inadmissible behavior." For his unduly zealous service to heaven and earth, Bishop Sergiy (Golubtsov), the administrator of the Novgorod and Staraya Russa Dioceses at the time, was issued a warning on Father Ilarion's account, and the bishop was finally forced to transfer him to serve at the Transfiguration of the Lord Church in the village of Bronnitsa, Novgorod Region. The city authorities would gladly have seen him sent farther, but Metropolitan Antony of Leningrad and Novgorod interceded on his behalf, and to Bronnitsa he went.

Nun Valentina remembered this time: "The evening before, as Father was praying with tears in his cell, the icon of the Vladimir Mother of God cracked.[6] He took this to be providential, and was calmed. The icon soon restored itself.

"In addition, several days before his new assignment, in a dream his cell attendant Anna saw the church in which Father was to serve, and told him: 'Do not be afraid, you will not be sent far—just 30 kilometers from Novgorod.' When she arrived in Bronnitsa with Father she recognized the church she had seen in her dream."

CHAPTER 8

Bronnitsa: The Birthing of Paradise

In Bronnitsa, too, Father Ilarion had to endure much, both from his own people and from strangers. Mother Valentina recalled how once, on Nativity, they had hardly broken the fast

---

For to me, to live is Christ, and to die is gain. . . .

For I am hard-pressed between the two, having a desire to depart and be with Christ, which is far better.[1]

---

at the festal meal when the phone rang: Father Ilarion was being summoned to the "corner house."[2] Calls like this were frequent. It became necessary to pay off the godless minions of the law, placating them with gifts and money.

From his first day in Bronnitsa to his last, Father was also given much grief by certain overzealous female followers who vied for position as his chief helpers. They mistook his generosity, gentility, compassion, and sympathy for their emotional and spiritual infirmities to be weakness. Yet, Father bore their cross on his own shoulders, pouring out for them the blood and pain of his wounded heart.

Time passed, and the period of Khrushchevian persecution of the Church gave way to the "stagnant era," which left its mark of desperation on all society.[3] Father Ilarion struggled with his emotional state in those minutes and hours of his life when he found himself unable to rise above the gloom that blanketed his soul. No news had been heard from Father for some time, and in alarm, Father Andronik inquired in a letter as to the reason for his silence.

A short reply dated April 30, 1978, bearing a scarcely legible signature (perhaps that of Archbishop Sergei) asked Father Andronik to take courage, to not lose heart, to rely on the aid of kind helpers, to remember his vows to God, to more frequently resort to the prayerful aid of the Mother of God, and to sweeten the hours of solitude with reading the writings of the Holy Fathers. The author went on to say, "only be more attentive to yourself, and manifest your pastoral zeal with greater care ... do not let yourself be caught in the subtle, craftily-woven net of the invisible foe." In a greeting card from Archbishop Sergei dated the following year, 1979, comforting Father Ilarion in his continued exile outside the monastery walls, the same bishop emphasized once again, "After all, one can also be saved in the world. Only be careful in your behavior, humbling yourself secretly."

The following excerpt is from an unsigned letter:

Dear brother in Christ of heartfelt remembrance Fr Ilarion!

My sincerest "May God save you!" for your words of greeting and Christly love expressed in your congratulatory telegram on the private Pascha of my life—my nameday.

Many read ... [illegible]. At our modest brotherly nameday meal Bp. Andrei, Vladyka Feodor, Archim. Afinogen, and many others mentioned you, wondering where you are and who you have become. Then all sang "Many Years." To be frank, they wish more for Your Very Reverence. I mean that they wish you what you deserve: the episcopacy.

During Christ's Nativity I spent four days in Leningrad (at the Academy), and nearly all the professors spoke of you and of how they tried to arrange for you to remain at the Academy. It is a joy to hear good, kind words, and to hear our monastic names and titles spoken and blessed.

In his 105th year, in January, Schemamonk Varsanufy (of the Glinsk Hermitage) reposed here. You know and remember him, no doubt?!

Father Ilarion also received a most well-disposed letter (undated) from Father Agafangel. There was no time to respond, nor was it in Father Ilarion's nature. He always found the courage to remain true to the Orthodox Church, continuing zealously to defend its interests. The spiritual flame in his eyes and his soul not only did not go out, but also burned ever brighter as the years went by.

The potency of Father's active nature was evinced first and foremost in his caretaking of the Bronnitsa church and its territory. He found the church in a shabby, pitiful state: loose plaster, broken windows, missing doors. There was no one to sing, no one to read, no one to light the censer. Gradually, however, with God's help, through Father Ilarion's care for the human souls entrusted to him, and by the zeal of spiritual children and benefactors, the church was restored. New buildings were erected, the vestry renovated and replenished, the icons and all the holy vessels restored, and the bell tower repaired. A choir was formed under the direction of Lyudmila Nikolaevna Sirota.

However, "the Church," according to the Holy Hierarch John Chrysostom, "is not roof and walls." Day in and day out, the service of the cross is performed in it, ensuring its welfare. Hence, along with the restoration efforts, prayer in the church never ceased. Services of need were regularly held, and fiery sermons resounded. From the very first days of his life in Bronnitsa, Father Ilarion strove to inculcate the best traditions of the Glinsk Hermitage, insomuch as was possible outside a monastery. A strict devotee of serving according to the typicon, he frequently performed the duties of chanter on the kliros, reader, and so forth.

Mother Galina Slukina of Veliky Novgorod described the transformation that occurred in Bronnitsa because of Father Ilarion. "We used to live in the village of Bronnitsa. In the church yard near the temple there was a small two-story wooden house, where the priests lived who served the parish. Archimandrite Ilarion was appointed rector of the church. Father Valentin had been serving here as second priest for about a year. Father Ilarion was transferred to this parish from Novgorod—an event about which he was not at all happy, and which upset him very much.

"Those were difficult times for church life. In Novgorod there was only one active church. The priest whom the Metropolitan assigned to the parish had to obtain a registration from the commissioner for religious affairs, and only then could he begin serving at the church. In the church, everything was run by parishioners elected to the so-called "twenty," who performed the duties of the warden or treasurer. These people had to answer to the commissioner and report to the diocese both on financial status and on everything that went on in the church. Sometimes these were pious and God-fearing people, and then peace and mutual understanding reigned in the parish. Some, however, became so accustomed to their post that they forgot who was really in charge at the church. These were capable of informing on a priest, and filing complaints which could result in his being transferred to a distant parish with no investigation whatsoever, or having his registration from the commissioner revoked, without which a priest could not serve in a single church in the Union.

"At Transfiguration of the Lord Church in the village of Bronnitsa there was considerable unrest. Complaints against priests were filed constantly, and the latter were replaced very frequently. It was after one such transfer that Father Ilarion was assigned as rector of this church. We had heard much of him.

"People predicted a great future for him, since our amazement knew no bounds when we learned that he served in the Church of the Apostle Philip in the city of Novgorod. And soon he was transferred to be rector in the village of Bronnitsa. It is most likely that by Divine Providence he was appointed to this parish as a peacemaker, being a person of great spiritual background.

"There was one domineering old lady who took account of no one, who had served as treasurer for over four decades. Priests meant nothing to her. 'I can have a different priest sent here within two days,' she used to say. 'But if the warden gets offended and leaves, we'll have to lock up the church.' To a certain degree, there was a grain of truth in her words. People were reluctant to work at the church. Problems could arise for such people at home. For this reason priests were very careful about how they treated the church workers, and tried to do everything to please them.

"All that changed when Father Ilarion arrived. His picturesque person, his ability to get along with people, his singing, and his attentiveness to everyone who entered the church changed everything in it. There were few regular parishioners, and he quickly became acquainted with everyone. He ignored the use of the formal patronymic in addressing people, and seemed to be the same age as everyone: 'Well, well, Katerina—you have a new skirt today! You were wearing a different one last time. And you, mother—didn't you have your barrette fastened differently last time...?' And so on, with a kind word for everyone—he missed nothing! Even if at first some people took offense, later on, like children, they were pleased by his attention. No one remained indifferent. Even our gruff old lady gradually got over her habits of glaring and preaching. It appeared that she sometimes saw in him her son who had died long ago, and felt the need to protect him from any unpleasantness and to take the best possible care of him. More often, however, she saw in him a father whom she wanted to mind and obey in everything. And so peace and respect for the priest gradually settled over the church. As for our old lady, who had been raised a Christian, she at last acquired the fear of God. She calmed down, gradually withdrew from all her duties, and remained a simple singer. She had a wonderful voice, and singing gave her considerable pleasure.

"At the time there was almost no one in the church who knew how to read, and the priests would alternate, with one serving and the other reading and singing on the kliros. Father Ilarion read magnificently, and loved to sing. During Great Lent the readings were particularly numerous, and he gave special attention during that time to reading the kathismata. If for any reason it was impossible to keep the rule entirely, Father would send his cell attendant to complete the entire reading at home.

"Father Valentin (Slukin) recalls that Father Ilarion had a great love for the Lenten services, and read the Great Canon of Saint Andrew of Crete with great feeling, making the choir repeat the irmoi, and always sang the kontakion from the canon himself, melodiously and prayerfully.

"Father Ilarion quickly resolved the problem of readers: he made everyone read, from singers to cleaning women. And he strictly took them to task for every mistake.

"'But Father, I'm a superintendent! I'm embarrassed to read by syllables,' one woman entreated him. 'Wait a little, and I'll practice a bit at home.'

"'Go on, read—you'll learn more quickly!' And learn she did.

"No one dared disobey him. Among workers, singers, and parishioners alike he enjoyed considerable authority and respect.

"Along with him arrived the sweet and kind Mother Anna, who lived with him in his house. It is likely that she was a secret nun.[4] Monasteries then were very few, and getting into them was incredibly difficult. So people took the tonsure secretly and lived either at a church or with priests, helping them around the parish and at home. Mother also helped Father around the house, preparing the meals and keeping the house in order. One could discern in her an aristocratic upbringing. Though always strict, she never raised her voice at anyone. She was welcoming and kind to all, could not abide flattery, and endeared herself to all by her reverent attitude towards Father Ilarion. Even on the day of Holy Pascha, while waiting for Father to return from the service, she would sweep every speck of dust from the outside steps with a rag, explaining to us that a priest's clothes should not touch dirt and dust.

"We lived in the same house as Father Ilarion. The house was wooden; its acoustics were superb. We were involuntary witnesses to his lengthy prayers and prostrations, which he made by the hundreds late in the evening, and would read the monastic rule for hours. He loved our children very much. He never spoke sternly to them: he talked with them as with adults, and never scolded them for a single one of their pranks.

"We lived together with Father Ilarion for ten years. He treated the second priest in a brotherly fashion, and was never arrogant or presumptuous. He always respected his rank, and tried not to offend him in any way.

"At last, however, the order came for our transfer to another parish. The day of our departure Father accompanied us out to the yard. We stood on the small porch outside his door. He bowed down to the ground before Father Valentin's feet, and both of them, on their knees and with tears in their eyes, asked forgiveness of one another. They rose and kissed each other thrice, then stood there, very downcast and at peace with one another. I also approached Father Ilarion to bid him farewell, and bowed to the ground before his feet. He answered by bowing from the waist, and imploringly asked: 'Mother, must I bow to the ground before you? After all, I am a priest!' I was moved to tears! Who was I, anyway, that such a priest should bow to me?

"Many decades have gone by since that day. Twice a year, until the very last year of his life, we would receive Father's greetings on the great feasts. Father Valentin recalls his years of serving with Father Ilarion with great respect and warmth.

"Our last meeting with him was in the summer of 2007 at St Sophia Cathedral, when all the priests of the diocese had gathered for the rite of the funeral of the Mother of God. Father Valentin is unwell, and uses a wheelchair. We stood at the side doors and waited for Archbishop Lev to arrive. All the clergy went out to meet him in their vestments. Father Ilarion went out as well; for some reason he was not vested. I had known that he was seriously ill, but words cannot describe what I saw. Before us stood an elder with a body entirely broken down, and extremely emaciated, yet who was somehow radiant throughout, quite vigorous, and very outgoing. He came over to us, greeted Father Valentin with a fatherly embrace, and tried very hard to comfort us."

Another remembrance of Father Ilarion's impact on Bronnitsa comes from Galina Petrovna Lashutina, of the village of Proletary:

"The first time I came to the Transfiguration of the Lord Church was on December 25/January 7, 1973, on the feast of Christ's Nativity. Archimandrite Father Amvrosy was serving at the time. In November of that year, however, Hegumen Father Ilarion appeared on the scene. From his first days of serving he seemed to me very strict and unusual. Every parishioner was at the center of his attention, and I, too, became its object. I was thirty-six at the time, and thanks to Father Ilarion I became a zealous attendee of the church services (although I had been going to church since I was seven). For some reason he immediately noticed me (probably because at the time there were almost no people as young as myself in the church). Approaching me, he invited me to talk. He was interested in everything: who I was, what my education had been, whether I was married, whether I had children, etc.

"Almost immediately after this lengthy conversation Father Ilarion invited me to confession. That was truly a complete revelation of both deeds and thoughts, and he offered me an obedience at the church.

"We all loved him very much for his strict kindness to us sinners. He could also be a little harsh, and on these rare occasions he would immediately run to ask forgiveness, saying: 'I will make (so many) prostrations for you; only forgive me.' He held nothing against anyone for even five minutes, and afterwards would come over again and again, and ask: 'Have you forgiven me?'...

"He spoke nothing but good of anyone, even if a person was a drunkard: 'That person is an angel of God, fallen prey to a savage and evil illness.' He even gave people money for coding,[5] and me— for travel to the holy places, but I always refused it. When a sizeable amount of money and valuables was stolen from him, in his humility he did not even report it to the police. The church's valuables, however, he guarded strictly....

"The number of tasks to be done under obedience were past comprehension: construction of a bathhouse, paving the territory around the church, laundering vestments (up to twenty-five at a time), a general laundering before every feast, and much more. Later came the construction and opening of a prosphora bakery (previously prosphora had been baked at home) and a Sunday school.

"Father was always a truly tireless laborer, a visionary, and our guide. He wanted to perfect everything in and around the church. He could not pray and serve at ease with disorder reigning supreme and the church in a state of neglect. Well I remember that unsettled environment.

"Considerable effort and thought were needed to establish at least some semblance of order to start with. It was a mystery how he could think through every task to the minutest detail. Only many years later did I understand just what spiritual power and wisdom he contained.

"There was no free time to speak of: only prayer, more prayer, and work. In his latter years he tried to do even more than before: he built a new public restroom facility (after tearing down the old, rotten one), overhauled the gatehouse and the two-story priests' house, and built a deep summit pump.

"Such thought and effort it took for an elderly man (over eighty years old) to labor this way! He did not boast of his elevation, and in every matter consulted myself and the others who served in the church. He did not feel his age, since the Holy Spirit and God's grace abode within him, and to some degree descended upon his spiritual children, as well. One could sense this clearly. Each year we would compile an annual report on the church at the Sunday school. He knew the answers to the items almost by heart; I could hardly write them down fast enough."

In the 1980s, after long years of persecution, the Church gained its freedom at last. It became clear that the country could not be resurrected without rousing faith in men's hearts, without returning to the source of our existence, Holy Orthodoxy. Father Ilarion saw the revival of the Church first and foremost as the revival of the violated holy things from atheistic nonentity, the enlightenment of his expanded flock with the light of Gospel truth. He constantly repeated the words of Saint Cyprian of Carthage: "He who does not have the Church as his mother does not have God as his father."[6]

The way Father Ilarion served in the church, according to the old Bronnitsa residents, particularly Capitolina Egorovna Paramonova, made an extraordinarily strong impression: "Father served the Divine Liturgy with deep reverence and ardent faith. During that time the whole church would fill with grace." Through the divine services, Father gave people the opportunity to feel the power of common prayer and the Church's sacraments. His brief exclamations (such as "Let us stand well, let us stand with fear," "Bow your heads unto the Lord," "Glory to Thee, O Christ God, our hope, glory to Thee") made their hearts tremble before the unsearchable mystery of the kingdom of God.

Each morning began with the singing of akathists: to Sweetest Jesus, the Protection of the Mother of God, and Holy Hierarch Nicholas the Wonder-worker. After the Liturgy, a moleben was sung. What strength of feeling lies in the church stichera, canons, other hymns, and the sacred liturgical rites! Without these, how dull, empty, and soulless is life with all its anxieties and commotion.

Father saw the Church as the keeper of enduring spiritual and moral values, historical memory, and cultural legacy. When praying with particular intensity, he felt in soul his kinship with the Lord, the Mother of God, the angelic world, and the holy saints of God. He tried to emulate them and live the life of grace in faith, love, and repentance. He rejoiced in this kinship and gave thanks to the Lord that, from his very birth, He had joined him to His Church and to the company of the saints.

Father Ilarion possessed an unearthly, naturally heavenly spirit. Often, fortunate as we were, we witnessed his ardent service at the liturgy and in his sermons. He lived in the Church and by the Church, by the word of God and its fulfillment, by the lives of the saints. He loved to read the menaion of the services, and the canons to the saints. Through him, all of us were drawn to heaven and into the church. The whole structure of our lives, both emotional and spiritual, was somehow special with Father—the way it should be but so rarely is.

On Saturday evening and Sunday morning, the stately melodies of the first tone, melding harmoniously with the texts expressing man's gratitude to Jesus Christ and sung with the light of Christ's resurrection, filled with the joy of the myrrh bearers, who were the first to learn that Christ had arisen. The next day—Sunday or some special feast—we invariably went to the Bronnitsa church and to Father for grace. He met everyone affectionately, greeted us with the feast, and removed particles from the prosphoron for our friends and relatives, both living and departed. If you came early, you might see a wedding as well, with everything snowy white and splendid, and Father Ilarion's homily wisely edifying and regal. The overall feeling would make one want to wed, to enjoy the splendor of the church and Father's wedding service.

When the service began, everyone stood in their assigned places—one on the kliros, another at the candle desk, another in his usual corner, and so forth—until they heard themselves called: "Come here for a minute." Father approached each person, saying something to each that concerned only him or her.

Then came the unforgettable moments of confession, which cannot be compared to any natural sauna—the heat penetrates to the very bone. Even if you had not prepared for communion, you unobtrusively slipped into line with the penitents. You stood there, seeing nothing around you, only listening and crossing yourself: "I am guilty, O Lord. Forgive me a sinner!" Then, all of a sudden, you heard, "What's this? You haven't fasted or prepared? No, no confessions for you. Go back and stand where you were." But then, a moment later: "Oh well, stand here like so and listen, so that maybe something will stir inside you, maybe your heart will turn to God and to the Church, maybe. Understand?"

Of course, the heart of the spiritual life for believers in Christ is the Eucharist—the supper of immortality, the "beginning of another existence." Through the window, beams of sunshine penetrated past the leaves of the trees. A special, auspicious silence pervaded the church. Only the chirping of the birds outside occasionally reached your ears. Through the open window top, splotches of sunshine penetrated through the leaves of the trees, intensifying the mysterious atmosphere. Then you heard Father's voice: "Thine own of Thine own, we offer unto Thee in behalf of all and for all," and all were immersed in the redeeming mystery of divine love.

The blessed minutes of holy Communion caused one's heart to stop as you approached the holy chalice, listening to the ethereal singing: "Receive ye the Body of Christ; taste ye of the Fountain of Immortality." One's soul was lifted up so high that you thought you were about to dissolve and disappear from the face of the earth. At such moments, one felt acutely that where there is no Communion, there is no communion with the New Life. There, as before, "death and time reign supreme on the earth."[7] A line by the poet Osip Mandelstam comes to mind: "And the Eucharist, as an eternal midday, lingers."

Oh, how Father read from the book of Epistles and from the Gospel! How he sang, and how he served molebens! If one waited around after the service, he might give you a prosphoron. You might even find yourself at a baptism and stand as godparent. Upon leaving the church, you would bow to it for the final time, as well as to your sister or brother in Christ.

All this, of course, is the wise institution of the Holy Spirit, the "Heavenly King, Comforter, and Spirit of Truth."[8] Without Father Ilarion's spiritual, grace-imbued guidance, however, we would have been incapable of being harnessed with this salvific team and of being held in soaring orbit, year after year, around the Church of God. I have neither the skill nor the spiritual energy to express the whirlpool of feelings and actions into which Father drew us, sweeping us away with the flame of his selfless love for God, Church, and neighbor.

To better express the sensations that filled us to overflowing, the following is an excerpt from the memoirs of Metropolitan Veniamin (Fedchenkov, 1880–1961), which superbly conveys the experiences we so clumsily and colorlessly describe:

> If you look back now, you see that all your life was intertwined with the Church. The Entry arrives, and already you hear the irmoi for Nativity: "Christ is born, Glorify Him!" Christmastide arrives, bringing with it a whole garland of feasts: the Nativity of Christ, Circumcision and New Year's Day, Theophany, St Basil the Great, and John the Baptist. The day before Nativity is Christmas Eve, and no eating until the first star; and on the eve of Theophany—no drinking before taking holy water.... Christmastide and the holy days have gone, and Cheesefare Week and Lent soon follow: the church bell ringing mournfully, dark vestments, fasting (fish was not to be eaten except on Annunciation and the Entry into Jerusalem), sincere confession, holy Communion.... And this for a month and a half. Then came the

overwhelming days of passion: the reading of the Twelve Gospels, the Shroud, the Burial of Christ.... And the midnight Bright Matins... Pascha! The Resurrection of Christ... Oh, God, what joy! A whole week of the bells pealing without stopping.

Soon came St George's Day: the cattle being driven out, molebens being served. The cows, grown lean over the winter, are sprinkled with holy water, and they go out to pasture to nibble the still-leaner grass. Ascension... Pentecost with its greens and flowers... Midsummer Day... Peter and Paul... another fast... the Kazan icon.... And already the first Savior is upon us, with its poppyseeds; and the second Savior—Transfiguration, with its apples (it is a sin to eat them before they have been blessed). The third fast, of the Dormition. The third Savior—the Icon Not-Made-By-Human-Hands.... The Beheading of the Forerunner. The Nativity of the Mother of God... The "Ascending," as the villagers called it, of the Lord's Cross. The autumn Kazan icon. Then another Entry... and another fast. And again the feasts go around for another whole year. And how many special saints there are in the year! The spring and summer St Nicholas, the Martyr Eudocia... St Mary of Egypt's Standing... Spyridon Midwinter (the winter solstice), Michael the Archangel, Ivan the Theologian, Gerasimus of Jordan with the lion (when the rooks came), Alexis the Man of God (larks were baked!), Cosmas and Damian (more than once each year)... Elias the Prophet (no working whatsoever, or he would punish you...), "Florus and Laurus and St Panteleimon" (the healers...). And so on for the entire year... And each Sunday is, in essence, a commemoration of Pascha.[9]

The way Father served the liturgies on Saturday of the first week of Great Lent and on Great Thursday, when all the parishioners would commune of the Holy Mysteries after fasting and fervent prayer, was memorably inspiring. Likewise, his prepaschal and paschal services were unforgettable.

Although in the majority of parish churches, to accommodate the weakness of the worshipers, the burial service is served late Friday evening, Metropolitan Veniamin (Fedchenkov) rightly noted that this practice is not overly inspiring: "The soul has not yet had time to break away from the thought of Christ's death. While the

Sunday troparia are already sung early Saturday morning, that is another matter. Then it is as though the soul awakens after a painful crisis, and rises to new life to meet the Resurrection. All these thoughts and feelings are not the fruit of theoretical musings, but rather the testimony of experience. And besides, is it really possible to be more discerning and judicious than the Church? It is the Church that moved the burial to Saturday morning." This is why Father Ilarion also served the burial early Saturday morning. We made our way to Bronnitsa however we could; some would come the previous evening to spend the night there, while others would come by car or hitchhike.

Once again, we convey the sensations we experienced through the words of Vladyka Veniamin:

> The sorrow was endured yesterday, on Friday.... There is no more strength left.... Only a quiet sadness remains. And yet, beneath it, life has already been secretly conceived: already, beyond the burial, His rising is ever more visible. He cannot remain in the tomb. Death is but the path to resurrection.... And the soul senses this, performing the unavoidable rite. And it is for this reason that suddenly, immediately after the mournful funeral, the glorious troparia of the myrrh bearers break forth: "Blessed art Thou, O Lord.... The assembly of the angels was amazed... the Savior is Risen...."
>
> The bright beam flashes...and disappears. Matins draws to a close. After the Great Doxology the shroud is carried around the church to the mournful, funereal singing of "Holy God." But the heart is at peace. It is morning... the sun is not yet risen, but already the sunrise has bathed the entire sky in jubilant colors. The fresh morning of the awakening day. The clear, cloudless (how one hopes!) sky...the twittering of the birds awakened from sleep....
>
> We have entered the church. For the final time, now without any trace of sorrow, we have sung "Noble Joseph"... and immediately begins the wondrous scriptural lesson on the bones that come to life.... How few people listen to it! Yet it is not just a prophecy of His resurrection, but of ours, as well....

The great day of rest.... The only Sabbath in the entire history of the world. Just as "God rested" after creating the world, so also the Word rested after rebuilding it through redemption. And with Him on this day all creation must also rest. "Let all mortal flesh keep silence," sings the Church. "This is the blessed Sabbath! This is the day of rest!"

We go our separate ways, each to his own house, to gather again that evening in the gaily arrayed church, this time for the festive Paschal Service, when the fullness of the beauty of the future age will unfold before us.

This is how the Transfiguration of the Lord Church in the village of Bronnitsa made ready to meet its Savior: the wondrous night, the flames of the candles, the solemn silence. The church was so full that you couldn't move your arms, and there were even more people in the churchyard and outside its walls. Tension built in expectation of the miracle. Then, from the altar, quiet chanting reached our ears: "Thy Resurrection, O Christ Savior...." In front, like apostles, came the priests carrying crosses, then all the men of the church carrying banners and icons, then the choir, and finally the parishioners with candles, like myrrh-bearing women. The procession around the church had begun.

Then, Father's greeting rang out: "Christ is risen!" In all human language, are there any words more life-giving and wonder-working than these, and those that followed: "Truly He is risen!"? The grace-imbued fire of this salvific news enlightened the Lord's tomb anew, suffusing our souls also with its bright light. The holy joy of the greatest feast of our Lord and Savior Jesus Christ had begun. The risen Christ walked upon the earth, the triumph of life over death! The immortality of the bright paschal joy pounded in our hearts.

Throughout the service, the priests came out by turns to cense at every ode. Again and again, the church resounded with the paschal exultation, "Christ is risen!" followed again and again by the exuberant response, "Truly He is risen!" This continued through all of Matins until the paschal greeting.

The paschal greeting, the blessing of paschal breads and colored eggs, the festal meal, the rainbow dancing of sunbeams in souls and in nature—everything was filled with rejoicing. The firmament filled with singing, chirping, cooing, and ringing. A little more, it seemed, and one's soul would break free from this earth out of unspeakable joy: "Christ is risen! Our sweetest joy!"

The Joy of Pascha

Glory and thanksgiving to the Resurrected Christ, Who has vouchsafed us this year once again to taste of the joy of His Resurrection! Christ is Risen, and life abides.

Now all things are filled with light: heaven and earth, and the nethermost parts of the earth!

Let us rejoice and be exceeding glad, for the Savior has brought us to the land of perfect joy!

Let us, then, you and I, receive into our hearts God's witness of our salvation!

Let us cling to the risen Christ!

Let us be radiant with the light of Christ!

Let us be renewed in spirit!

Let us discover for ourselves that there are other cares, more befitting for man than cares . . . for the one thing needful to the stomach—cares for the life of the spirit!

Let us ponder our lot beyond the grave, our eternal and immortal soul!

Let us begin building our life upon other foundations, gathering our heavenly riches into earthly garners!

Let us make our whole life a service to God, as did Christ the Savior!

Around six o'clock in the morning, we departed for our homes. Guests from away bedded down for the night wherever they must, as weariness had taken its toll. Yet, through the sweet half-sleep, one upon another, came the sounds of the festal greetings from Father Ilarion's sermons and the paschal services, obliging the soul to tirelessly give thanks, to glorify God, and having caught its breath, to labor day and night, day and night.

Oh, Father Ilarion, how good and wonderful it is that you were with us, that you are with us, and that you will always be with us! What a sharp blade you were across our hearts, and what a bittersweet mark you left in them. With what longing the bitterness of your loss to the earth's bounds rings in our hearts, and how sweetly our hearts are wrenched by the foretaste of a possible meeting to come!

The following verses were written by one of Father's spiritual children.[10] This song was performed by the children of the Sunday school at a paschal children's performance [Spring 2008] and is now frequently sung in the Bronnitsa church.

Grateful I am to you, Mother of God,

Who to Bronnitsa showed me the road.

Its beautiful places and plentiful forests

In heavenly gift you bestowed.

Refrain:

Here to school I went,

Here I happiness found,

Here I learned to know sorrow and joy.

And people I met, and my children I raised,

And ideas no end did employ.

Merciful Mother, Birthgiver of God,

Our Bronnitsa do not forsake.

With goodness surround us and show us the path,

And support all that we undertake.

Refrain:

And in church let the people pray earnestly

for Bronnitsa's health as is meet.

Let the birds build their nests, and let people and beasts

Inside every man's heart find retreat.

In 1997, Father Ilarion fell seriously ill. With each day, he grew steadily worse. He was literally wasting away before the very eyes of his multitudinous flock. He looked frighteningly gaunt and pale. His body rejected all food. For the first time, his spiritual children saw him lying in bed, his face drawn. To everyone, it seemed that they were seeing him for the last time. When he spoke to them, they took his words as a final farewell, a parting testament.

Metropolitan Anthony of Sourozh provided consoling words on facing one's demise:

> We know nothing about death. We do not know what happens to us at the moment of dying, but we have at least some concept of what eternal life is. Each of us knows from experience that there are certain moments when one lives not in time, but in a fullness of life and a rejoicing that are not entirely of this world. Hence, the first thing we must teach ourselves and others is to prepare not for death, but for life.
>
> And, if we do speak of death, to speak of it only as a door that will open wide and allow us to enter into eternal life.

In a short space of time, Father Ilarion underwent one operation after another, but almost no hope of recovery remained. On the day of his funeral, ten years later, Archbishop Lev recalled this troubled time: The attending physician informed him of Father Ilarion's inevitable, sorrowful departure, and Archbishop Lev went to him in Bronnitsa to prepare him. During this visit, Father Ilarion said, "All things are by God's providence, Vladyka."

The ardent prayers of all for the health of their dear Father Ilarion inclined the Lord to mercy. Although the illness never left him, and his body suffered constantly, he was stronger in spirit than ever before, calling to mind Christ the Savior's words to the holy Apostle Paul: "My grace is sufficient for you, for My strength is made perfect in weakness."[11]

It was in this condition of extreme physical infirmity that, to the amazement of all, Father Ilarion fulfilled his cherished wish of making a pilgrimage to the Holy Land. I recall how, during the sermon at St Sophia Cathedral during Holy Week, we heard words spoken in sympathy for the gravely ill Father Ilarion, requesting our ardent prayers that he quickly regain his health and rise from his bed. At that very moment, Father Ilarion was flying in spirit over the hills of Palestine, exhausting his body by such ascents on high that he would have been in serious trouble with his physician if he had known. Naturally, Father asked the bishop's blessing on his intention to make such a lengthy journey, although his health had so sharply deteriorated that no one could have imagined that his intention would be realized.

In 2000, he again made plans to travel to the Holy Land. The doctors, however, did not approve such a long trip and insisted on his hospitalization. Father Ilarion counted the days and hours of his time in the hospital, assuring the medical personnel that he was feeling better, and that he would run away regardless. The cardiogram was no respecter of persons, however, as Father Ilarion had suffered a heart attack.

Svetlana Borisovna, the department head, was obliged to wage battle with her disobedient patient to keep him on his hospital cot and off the hills of Palestine. She sternly announced that Father Ilarion would leave the hospital only over her dead body. The airline ticket was returned, and the second pilgrimage to the promised land was never made. Father Ilarion felt himself an unhappy child, from whom something infinitely dear had been confiscated.

Despite his physical ailments, however, he continued to live in the interests of the church and his flock. He gave himself up entirely to serving his neighbors, striving to comfort, support, and instruct them. He was present at all the divine services, serving, confessing, and communing, and until his final day, he performed all the church services of need.

He felt that every day was a mercy shown him by God and did not spare his strength, which was being rapidly depleted by his exhausting illnesses and labors, dedicating even his nocturnal hours to the work of his pastoral calling. Whether he lived or died did not matter to him. What mattered was what he lived for and for what cause he would die. Under the strain, his heart began to give out. Father Ilarion took his medication and continued to serve. There were times when he would lose consciousness and fall; yet, upon regaining his senses, he would once again engage in the service. It was painful to look at him, his legs swollen like logs and covered with ulcers, his eyes hollow. During the service, however, he would be in such high spirits that one involuntarily forgot his age and sickness. At times, he seemed an ardent youth. Never for a moment could one imagine him motionless, with lips silent, not calling on the Lord, not giving praise to Him.

He was always in action and taught those around him to constantly compel themselves to God-pleasing work. He selflessly and devotedly bore his own illnesses and the burden of the moral illnesses of his spiritual children. He prayed much for those he confessed, bringing them by his wise instruction and, more importantly, by his profound insight into the recesses of the human soul, to recognition of their guilt and contrite repentance.

Father Ilarion had always slept little, and, in the last few years, he began sleeping not more than two hours, at times not sleeping even a wink. Gennady, the guard, often saw the light in Father Ilarion's window burning through the night and heard thuds on the floor. For a long time, Gennady thought that it must be Father Ilarion falling from his chair at night. Once, however, after listening closely, Gennady realized that Father Ilarion was making prostrations. When he did happen to sleep a little, the guard would often hear sudden cries from Father, crying out in his sleep from pain.

Here, we turn to letters of this period from Father's spiritual children:

> In Father I saw a person who lived for God. His service to God was greater than his illnesses. Though they tormented him every hour, there was not a single illness that could break his God-bearing spirit. Nothing could hold him back or subject him to inaction. In spite of all natural laws, disregarding the ominous diagnoses, with his last ounce of strength he strove to serve God, and ardently loved everything that was of God.[12]

> We received your letter and Father's photo. We could not refrain from tears—when was he so ill, so barely alive? After an operation, perhaps? Our dear Father and martyr ... now he is ill, aged,

and helpless, yet he endures everything, and humbles himself.... There are many of us, but only one Father. How we must pity and care for him, how sick and weak he is! He has crucified himself entirely for us sinners.[13]

I am very worried about Father; he is so sick and thin. How and with what can I help? Only with prayer! We all pity him greatly and pray for him![14]

Increase, O Lord, Father's spiritual and bodily strength, and raise him up from his bed of sickness. His legs are swollen; Father served three days in a row. Dear Father, forgive us, your sinful, disobedient children.[15]

How we all pity Father, with all the trials, sorrows, and sicknesses he has endured.[16]

In early May of 2008, accompanied by his cell attendant Mother Valentina, Father Ilarion left for an examination in Moscow at the N. N. Burdenko Neurosurgical Institute. It was Great Lent, and for this reason, before completing even ten days of treatment, he hurried back to his church in Bronnitsa and his parishioners, promising the physicians to return shortly. Circumstances would not permit him to return to the clinic, however, as the spring of 2008 was Father Ilarion's last. In the hospital in Moscow, he confessed to Vladyka Nikon, who was serving with the blessing of His Holiness the Patriarch at one of the Moscow churches, "all my sins from my very youth." Of this full confession, Father Ilarion was very glad.

Upon returning to Bronnitsa, Father Ilarion continued to attend all the divine services, although only on feasts was he able to preside. Sensing that the last of his strength was deserting him, he was now unable to fast the entire first week of Lent, and on Wednesday, he drank hot water with a spoonful of honey. He then ate nothing more until Saturday.

Father Ilarion's very presence in the church was invigorating for everyone, and gave them their second wind. People tried not to bother him with their needs, as it was enough to know that he was in church, to hear his exclamations, jokes, and reproofs. Everything from him was balm to the spirit: Father Ilarion was alive and on his feet! Glory to Thee, O Lord, our Lord! God willing, our dear Father would go on living, and the parishoners smiled happily, exchanging glances.

Father Ilarion's zeal for God covered everyone entirely, it seemed, with his inspired protection, but he was growing ever weaker. His lost health was now beyond repair, and his system could not withstand the constant stress, the sleepless nights, the physical strain. Yet, he felt obliged to serve all the services of need himself on his days to serve, just as though he were in perfect health. He now came to the church supported on either side and was led back the same way. Sometimes he would stand with eyes closed and bowed head at the iron rail, and when things were completely beyond endurance, he would lean slightly against it. Sometimes he would sit on a chair while holding the cross to be kissed.

As his physical strength deserted him, he became increasingly gentle and lenient. His exhausted flesh, it seemed, could not keep up with his spirit, which burned now with an otherworldly fire, floating as though outside the body. It seemed that for his thoughts and feelings, there no longer existed any natural obstacles. He had glimpsed eternity, and enraptured by what he had seen, he now saw everything with eyes no longer physical, and moved about not on his invalid legs but by pure strength of will.

Foreseeing the bitter loss, the whole church prayed to the Lord: let this cup of sorrow pass by us all. Yet, the time came of which the psalmist said, "As for man, his days are like grass; as a flower of the field, so he flourishes."[17] Along with Holy Hierarch Tikhon of Zadonsk, Father could have said, "Thy hands have made me and fashioned me, O Lord! I was an infant—and it escaped me; a child I was—and it passed me by. I was a young man—and it slipped away from me. A man I was, whole and strong—this too escaped me. Now my hair groweth gray and with old age I fail, yet even this passeth, and approacheth the end, and I shall go the way of all the earth. I was born that I might die. I die that I may live. Remember me, O Lord, in Thy Kingdom!"[18]

On Sunday, May 25, Father Ilarion administered the final examinations at the Sunday school. He was in good spirits and did not so much examine the children as teach, instruct, and inspire them. Igor Kornilyev, a Sunday school graduate, recalled,

Father held and still holds an important place in my soul. The best days and years of my life are connected with him. Today, however, along with the day I first saw Father, I see with particular clarity the last day I saw Father alive, at the final exam in our Sunday school. Father was in high spirits: he asked the children many things, and was very pleased that the school he loved so much had successfully completed yet another academic year, and that he had graduated another twenty-two persons—our largest graduating class ever.

Father was not well that day, but somehow he was especially tender and affectionate with the children, giving presents to all and blessing their future successes in their studies and work. One could sense that he did not wish to leave, and he began telling the children and adults who remained in the classroom a remarkable story from his life: once, when he was little, he was sitting at lunch with his parents. As he reached for the porridge bowl with his spoon, suddenly a star like the star of Bethlehem illumined the table. His parents exchanged glances: both had the thought that this was no accident. When he went out to the porch, the star illuminated him completely. It occurred to him then that he would need much strength, courage, and zeal on the path to God. Naturally, this story touched every one of us.

On Monday, Father had a slight cold. That day, and on Tuesday and Wednesday, he directed the workers in the churchyard from the open window of his house. Possibly, he already sensed his end

For I am hard-pressed between the two, having a desire to depart and be with Christ, which is far better. Nevertheless to remain in the flesh is more needful for you. And being confident of this, I know that I shall remain and continue with you all for your progress and joy of faith.[19]

Ready is my heart, O God, ready is my heart.[20]

approaching, and like many of the Glinsk elders, he foretold it. Not long before, he had cryptically mentioned this to one of his spiritual daughters. She had asked a blessing to come to him on Pascha, and Father had replied, "You will come on terrible Saturday." She thought he was referring to Holy Saturday, which would not be until 2009. However, on Saturday, May 31, 2008, that "terrible Saturday" for all of Father Ilarion's children, she came to him from St Petersburg for his funeral.

I want nothing more in this whole world,

Only give to me a candle, Lord,

That until the hour of death occurs

Its small quiet flame I might preserve.

And when in the early morning hours

I am called to go into Thy house,

In Thy silence, out of sight of men,

Do Thou take the candle from my hands.[21]

The entire final year was an extremely anxious one for all who loved Father Ilarion. It seemed that he was no longer here on earth, that he had already prepared for a new life, for the life which "beginneth once, but will never end—it will be unceasing and unchanging."[22] Mother Alexandra related how, on the day of his repose, Father Ilarion commanded her not to leave ("Sit by me; if you leave, I'll die alone without you").

Nikolai Dmitrievich Drozd, a surgeon in Veliky Novgorod, recalled Father Ilarion's final days: "When I first saw Father five years ago, there was no way I could have supposed that I would be the last person he would converse with in the bounds of his earthly life, and become a witness to his death. In the morning, on Sunday, May 25, Father approached me in the church and said: 'Just look how alive I am. That's because I confessed while I was in Moscow. And now I feel well, even though the Moscow doctors told me: 'We can't get you back up on your feet, Father, but we'll keep your heart going a little.' But look, I'm walking! The swelling has gone down a little. Don't wait for me; today I'm going to the school to grade the children's exams.'

"On the evening of May 26 I called Father and asked a blessing to travel to St Petersburg for continuing education courses. He blessed me, but complained of feeling poorly. He was tired, and, according to Capitolina Egorovna, had caught cold. 'Well, but you'll be here on the weekend?' Father asked, to which I nodded affirmatively and told him which medications he needed to take, and that he needed to contact the regional hospital and have them come and listen to him. Father, however, categorically refused. The morning of May 28 my wife called and told me that Father was doing very poorly. I reached Father Ilarion by telephone and offered to have him hospitalized at the regional hospital. His answer was a categorical refusal, and he asked me to come: he would wait for my arrival, and then we would decide together what was to be done next. Something made me hurry, however, and at noon the same day I left St Petersburg by bus.

"Upon arriving in Novgorod I called Bronnitsa, but no one answered the phone. On Thursday morning I contacted one of Father's spiritual daughters, who told me that he was sick, and was waiting for Georgiy (the stomatologist) and myself. We immediately left for Bronnitsa (around five or six o'clock in the evening). We drove up to the church and found the gates locked, making it practically impossible to reach the house. No one answered our phone calls. At last Fr Vladimir heard us calling, and led us through his yard to Father's house, where we were met by Mother Alexandra. Father was sitting on the bed in his cell. His breathing was shallow, his face pale, and his body damp. He half-opened his eyes, blessed us, and asked: 'So you've flown in at last, my doves?'

"Seeing Father's serious condition, I offered to call him an ambulance and take him straight to the hospital. He refused, however, saying that we should wait until morning, since in the morning he always felt better. But his blood pressure was barely registering, his pulse could not be felt, and without his permission I left his cell to call the hospital. In a few minutes, however, Mother Alexandra called me to Father, whose breath had practically stopped; his breathing and heartbeat were inaudible. Thus our dear Father went to the Lord before our very eyes.

"Two or three weeks before his repose he had been planning to come to Moscow, to the physicians, and he asked me several times: 'What should I do about Moscow?' 'Go, Father,' I said. 'But who will I leave here?' 'Someone will look after the house; don't worry.' But he waved me off. Of course, if his cell attendant Valentina had been here he would have held on a little longer, but his heart was already giving out. When his lungs were last X-rayed, the aorta resembled a dried-up brooklet. The air was barely filtering through the narrow fissure.

"After Father's repose you feel yourself an orphan. But one joy remains: conversing with him at his grave. You talk with Father as though he were alive, and you feel easier at heart.

"Grant eternal rest, O Lord, to Archimandrite Ilarion who loved Thee."

The Lord called His faithful laborer and ascetic of the Orthodox faith to Himself. Father Ilarion, "full of days,"[23] passed over the threshold of his earthly life at nine o'clock in the evening on May 29, 2008.

It should be noted that the Gospel read in the church that day was from the sixth chapter of John, on the feeding of the five thousand with five loaves of bread. The reading for the second day was from the ninth and tenth chapters, where the Lord calls Himself "the door of the sheep."[24] In light of Father Ilarion's repose, the Gospel texts were involuntarily illuminated with additional profound meaning, linked closely to his person.

In leaving this earthly life, Father Ilarion took care to strengthen the faith in Christ of those in need, over and over giving them the opportunity to see through this parable that spiritual hunger cannot be satisfied in the usual way, and that one ought to live first and foremost by one's daily bread.[25] This idea is continued in chapters nine and ten, where it is said that only in Christ can one find healing from spiritual blindness. He is "the light of the world,"[26] and to those who seek Him, He gives the light of life, while to those who reject Him, He will bring judgment, in that they will remain in the darkness of ignorance and sin.[27]

The tenth chapter introduces the parable of the hireling pastor, who is negligent in his treatment of the flock entrusted to him, and of the pastor who takes every care for his sheep. The Lord calls Himself "the door" leading to "the sheep," not over the fence, and "the sheep hear His voice." He "leads them out" to pasture and He goes before them, showing them the path, laying down His life for them as a good pastor, while the wolf (the usurping ruler) spiritually catches the sheep and scatters them.[28]

We, Father Ilarion's spiritual children, felt like just such "sheep," whom for many years he led through the door of grace, opened for us in Christ, Who said of Himself, "I am the door. If anyone enters by Me, he will be saved."[29] Father helped us go through this door by his living and active faith in Christ, the Son of God. Faith cannot be taught, as Father Andronik, his spiritual father, said. Faith is a gift from God. Whoever has become a partaker of this grace-imbued gift and preserves it in himself "will not sleep unto death," even in the grave.

Yet, the day came when, from the lips of the church hymnographer, we heard, "Come, brethren, let us give the last kiss to the dead, rendering thanks unto God." All night long, the body of the reposed lay in Father Ilarion's cell. After he had been robed in the appropriate vestments, the first pannykhida was served for the departed pastor. The Gospel was read ceaselessly.

At noon, the coffin holding Father Ilarion's body was carried into the church where he had served for thirty-four years. In that time, he had served thousands of funerals and comforted thousands of people in their final hour, conveying to them his faith and his heartfelt warmth unto eternal life and the mercy of God.

Those who first crossed the threshold of the Transfiguration of the Lord Church twenty or thirty years ago found Father Ilarion full of strength and energy. It seemed that he was endowed with immortality, that he would never die and never leave in sorrow those who entrusted their souls to him. Yet, here he was, lying motionless before the altar of God: "Now I have reposed and found great rest, for I have departed from incorruption, and clung to life."

Nothing offers any comfort, nothing dulls the sharp pain of irreparable loss: "O death, how bitter is the memory of you."[30] Only unceasing prayer reminds one that Father Ilarion's parting from the earth and from us is the day of his birth unto a new life, eternal and everlasting, and offers hope for a meeting to come, which then will never end. We must not, and we will not, grieve at the beloved coffin "as others who have no hope."[31]

Oh, Father, how many people you gathered about you! Your spiritual children from Russia, Belarus, and Ukraine flocked to you for the final parting and kiss; bowing the knee, they pray for your repose "in the heavenly abodes of the righteous," begging you for forgiveness and offering belated repentance, for you hear them and understand and accept them. What heavy crosses you bore, both your own and the crosses of your spiritual children, bearing the chronicle of our sins in your pastoral heart to that far country from which you will never return to us.

Some of us were brought to despair by our sins against you and before God, especially when we learned of your prostrations by the thousands each week for us wretched ones, who at times took offense at you for an unbiased word, reproach, or glance. Yet, even now it is not too late for each of us to correct ourselves, straighten our crooked path in life, and beg God for forgiveness for the sake our dear Father Ilarion. If we do not, all his selfless labors in the work of our salvation are fruitless and in vain.

At Father Ilarion's coffin, pannykhidas, All-Night Vigils for the departed (Parastasas), and litiyas were served. All the clergy from the Novgorod Diocese came to accompany Father Ilarion on his final journey, headed by the ruling bishop Lev of Staraya Russa and Novgorod, who in company with Archbishop Luka of Glukhov and Konotop and representatives of the diocesan clergy served the Divine Liturgy and the paschal rite funeral on May 31, 2008. The deep sorrow of the clergy, laity, and spiritual children gathered at the coffin gave way after the memorial service to triumphant glorification of Christ who rose from the dead and opened the dwellings of paradise, to which the soul of the reposed had been lifted up to behold the glory of the Savior of men. The words of Archpriest

Alexander Shargunov came to mind: "If we did not die, we would have nothing to do with His death and, consequently, His Resurrection." Sorrow gave way to paschal joy and the faith that Father was now with the Lord in eternal Pascha.[32]

At the end of the Divine Liturgy, Archbishop Lev expressed his profound condolences to the Novgorod Diocese, the parishioners of the church, and the spiritual children of the reposed, and spoke in his address of the elder's pious life and lofty pastoral labor. A heartfelt address on Father Ilarion's time in the Glinsk Hermitage, and his ardent spirit, which inflamed the hearts of men with heavenly fire, was given by the monastery superior Archbishop Luka of Belgorod and Konotop.

The clergy reverently carried the coffin containing the body of our reposed Father around the altar, according to the rite of priestly burial, and then around the church. After this, the parting procession boarded buses and left for the burial site at the Khutyn Monastery cemetery, where they were met by a large assembly of people. Following a short litiya, the coffin was lowered into the grave to the singing of "Memory Eternal." The memory of Father Ilarion will live always in the hearts and prayers of many, for "love never fails."[33]

◆ ◆ ◆

Archbishop Luka's Funeral Address for Father Ilarion

Your eminence, right worthy Vladyka Lev! Beloved brothers and sisters in the Lord!

Christ is Risen!

The Apostle Paul commands us: Bear ye one another's burdens, and so fulfill the law of Christ....Today we all accompany our dear Father Ilarion on his final journey. Hence, beholding his earthly life, we can say that he bore our burdens, and thereby fulfilled the law of Christ.

At a young age Father became a monastic in the Glinsk Hermitage. For over ten years he labored in this holy monastery, where with patience and humility he fulfilled the law of Christ.

While yet in the Glinsk Hermitage he often loved to tell newly-tonsured monks: "Brother, preserve the grace which you received at your tonsure." He would relate how he felt the presence of this grace, this wondrous help from the Lord, for a full three years after his tonsure.

By God's will, after the monastery was closed, Father found himself in the region of Novgorod where he continued to fulfill the law of Christ. In spite of the persecutions which he underwent, unafraid of what was happening in the country during the Soviet era, and of what they attempted to do to the Church in the 1960s, Father stood firmly in the faith of Christ. Moreover, he did not desert all those who came running to him for help, for advice and prayer.

Beloved brothers and sisters in the Lord!

Our eyes swim with tears, and our hearts brim with sorrow, because one dear to us has left this earthly life.

I never conversed with Father in person; we conversed only by telephone. Yet we try to fulfill his advice and instruction at, as he used to say, "our lovely lady the Glinsk Hermitage." He carried this love for the Glinsk Hermitage throughout his entire life. Here he conversed with Venerable Seraphim (Amelin), Father Seraphim (Romantsov), and Father Andronik, his spiritual father, to whom he revealed the secrets of his heart. He wonderfully fulfilled the blessing of his spiritual father, and never murmured against life.

He likewise conversed with the greatest elder not only of our own Church, but of the Georgian Church as well: Schema-Metropolitan Seraphim (Mazhuga). This glorious host of wondrous holy ascetics of God (I am not afraid to say words, since our monastery has compiled materials on their lives and submitted them to the Ukrainian Orthodox Church's commission for glorification of saints) had a tremendous influence on the spiritual formation of the young monk Father Ilarion.

When Father recalled his monastery, he always wept and said: "How I wish I would grow wings, and that I could fly to my monastery—my lovely lady the Glinsk Hermitage."

It is difficult for us to imagine how difficult it is to endure nostalgia for the home of one's birth. In addition to our coming to Father with our sorrows and problems, receiving comfort and support from him, he also endured his own inner sorrow:

nostalgia for the home of his birth, his monastery. He sorrowed uncomplainingly, but with tears in his eyes. We should not cry today, since we hear the call on behalf of the reposed (from the funeral rite for a clergyman): "Weep not." For Father has gone to another life, the life eternal.

Today, kissing Father Ilarion for the last time, we must for all time save and preserve in our hearts love not only for Father, but also for what he taught us: faith in Christ, the commandments of God, love for the Lord and our neighbor, patience, and humility, showing this by our life's example.

Today the Holy Church commemorates Venerable Macarius (Glukharev),[33] enlightener of the outlying Altai Region, who was likewise a brother of the Glinsk Hermitage, a child of its tonsure. Hence, I am certain that Venerable Macarius together with the angels will be a helper to Father Ilarion as he passes through the tollhouses, and will lead his soul to the throne of God, interceding for it before God. And that there, before the throne of God, they will pray together for us living here on earth.

Our parting is not for long—only for the time which the Lord has measured for us to be here, on the earth, that we might continue to prepare our souls for eternal life, fulfilling the commandments of God and the law of Christ.

Vladyka Lev said today that Father may be called an elder. An elder, then, is not a person who is very old, but rather one who by his wisdom, spiritual life, and spiritual labor shows us the way to the Lord.

Dear Father! On behalf of all the brethren of "the lovely lady the Glinsk Hermitage," I ask your forgiveness if we have offended you in any way. I assure you that we will strive to fulfill the testaments you have given us. I also ask your support and prayers at the throne of God for our monastery, that with God's help and beneath the omophorion of the Mother of God it might prosper not only materially, but also spiritually, and that its brethren, beholding your own life's path and that of the other Glinsk ascetics, might correct their lives and inherit the Heavenly Father's "royal mansions of paradise." Amen."

CHAPTER 9

Asleep in the Body, but Alive in God

The ninth day after Father Ilarion's death fell on May 23/June 5, the Feast of the Ascension of the Lord, and the fortieth day was June 24/July 7, the Feast of the Nativity of the Honorable and Glorious Prophet and Forerunner John, the Baptizer of the Lord, who is Father's patron saint. On the latter day, he would have turned eighty-four years old.

Archpriest Alexander (Ranne), a cleric of St Sophia Cathedral, gave an earnest address on the ninth day after Father Ilarion's death:

> During a very difficult time, Father Ilarion dedicated himself to serving the Church and preaching the Gospel. He turned away from the entire world, like those in ancient times who decided that worldly life strays too far from truth, and he left worldly life at a time when to declare oneself a Christian was to become a confessor.
>
> He knew that in those times priests were being shot not merely by tens, but by thousands. In our Novgorodian land in 1937, all the priests were shot. These, then, were the times in which he left everything and became a monk.
>
> After a monastery was closed, the monks would be shot. It is unknown why the monks were not shot after all the monasteries in the Novgorodian land were closed. It is a wonder how Father Ilarion remained among the living.
>
> When the God-hating atheist government in our country came to an end, he was one of the first to open a Sunday school for children, and not merely open one—he built a spacious theo-logical school on the foundation of an old cabin, invited university

lecturers, and gathered children from the families of alcoholics from all over, who did not know where to lay their heads. They came to the school in buses, and came to the church services, where they were baptized, taught, and fed free of charge. Father Ilarion would come to them after the service, work with them, listen to them, and give them spiritual and moral instruction. He lived entirely by this labor of ministry to these little ones. The kingdom of heaven abode in his soul, and he wished to sow it in the souls of these little people.

And now today, on the ninth day since Father Ilarion's departure, we pray for his soul, that the Lord may have mercy upon him, and upon us sinners. We hope that as a member of Christ's Heavenly Church he will offer up his holy prayers for us to the Lord.

On the fortieth day of Father Ilarion's repose, a memorial liturgy was served in the church of the Khutyn Monastery, after which Vladyka Luka addressed all the worshipers with deep concern and sympathy. He characterized Father Ilarion as a person of genuinely Christian soul, a humble laborer, and a grace-imbued intercessor in the Lord's field.

At the graveside pannykhida, Archimandrite Sophrony, from the Glinsk Hermitage, read several poems written and dedicated to our dear Father by his spiritual daughter Anna Ivanovna Zhuravleva, from the city of Pechora, which expressed the feelings of all who had gathered to visit Father Ilarion. Here is one of them:

When there come times hard to bear,

At his photograph I gaze—

Grace I feel upon my heart,

And I feel my sorrow eased.

Ever is he by my side,

Pastor good, and servant, too,

By his prayer preserving us

From the never-sleeping foe.

To his prayer the Lord does hearken,

Sending grace from up above.

Father takes the Spirit's gifts,

Bestowing them upon his children.

Ever-memorable and dear,

He, the flower, we, the bees.

God's nectar he gives us to drink,

Pursuing godly industry!

Anna Ivanovna Zhuravleva later recalled this time:

The last night, on the fortieth day, two fathers from the Glinsk Hermitage slept in Father's cell, while the rest of us slept in the hall on the floor. It was our final evening, and it was so touching, so melancholy, and at the same time we were happy for Father—he had been away, our dear one, and now he had returned to his native home.

Dear Father, how much you endured from us sinners, and forgave everything with love. How dull and hard it is without you! No one will stroke and comfort us; only your grave unites us all, scattered over hill and dale throughout the country.

For many, losing Father Ilarion proved a bereavement that nothing and no one could fill. During the forty days, when the Lord gave them special strength through Father, it was easier to bear the terrible loss. Since then, however, with each day, it becomes increasingly acute and painful to not have our sweet, dear Father by our side, for the lips to be closed that had once roused you at the crack of dawn over the telephone, and the hands that had worked good so bountifully to be crossed on his breast, covered with earth. The one comfort is that he has not died but has departed, going the "way of all the earth,"[1] to a world incomparably better. The Savior Himself called death a dormition, or sleep ("Our friend Lazarus sleeps"[2]). When the disciples did not understand what He was saying, He explained to them that "Lazarus is dead."[3]

It was in the Old Testament, as the Apostle Paul explained, that "death reigned,"[4] not yet having been conquered by Christ's life-creating death. But in the New Testament, "Christ died for us,"[5] and we "were reconciled to God through the death of His Son."[6] Being rich in mercy, God so loved us that those who die with Christ "in Christ all shall be made alive"[7] after death. How many times we heard these words of the Gospel in Father Ilarion's sermons, and how comfortingly they now touch our hearts, now that we have seen him off on this long, mysterious path of no return.

"'Blessed are the dead who die in the Lord from now on.' 'Yes,' says the Spirit, 'that they may rest from their labors, and their works follow them.'"[8] Our dear father is alive in God; he has fallen asleep in the body, but his soul, as always, is nearby and dear to all who knew and love him. Let us not disturb our beloved Father Ilarion's eternal repose with laments. With hope, out of love, and with reverent memory, let us remember his life and works, like him remaining vigorous in spirit and clear in mind, and always, as he and the Glinsk elders taught, maintaining remembrance of death and fear of the judgment to come.

CHAPTER 10

The Beauty of Immortality

A new epoch—"the epoch," in the words of Saint Ignatius (Brianchaninov), "that marks the beginning of our real life"—began for Father Ilarion's spiritual children in the year after his death. Only last year, we celebrated the Ascension of the Lord and the feasts of the Holy Trinity and the Holy Spirit, and listened to his exhortation before Saint Peter's Fast. After his repose, the events of the church calendar seemed to have taken on an additional, somewhat bitter meaning.

For the first time, at the great entrance in the Transfiguration of the Lord Church in Bronnitsa, instead of "our all-honorable father, the Reverend Archimandrite Ilarion together with the brethren of this holy monastery," we heard commemorated, "The reposed, newly departed Reverend Archimandrite Ilarion may the Lord God remember in His kingdom always, now and ever, and unto the ages of ages."

For the first time without Father Ilarion, we celebrated the Feast of the Holy Leaders of the Apostles Peter and Paul, which he had served particularly festively, and after which he would always leave on vacation. By the Feast of Holy Great-Martyr and Healer Panteleimon, he was always back in his place. Everyone would be eagerly awaiting him and would hurry to Bronnitsa for the service. This time, however, on August 9, 2008, the parishoners of the Bronnitsa church celebrated the feast without him.

The first Dormition Fast passed without Father Ilarion's intense prayers and blessings, for whom and in what ways the fast could (or could not) be relaxed and who, on the contrary, could keep it more strictly. At the first parish feast, the Transfiguration of the Lord, that was celebrated without Father, we stood at his grave and wondered, Where is he now, our dear one—in Bronnitsa or in Khutyn? for in both places, it was the parish feast. Touching the soul of each person praying there, Father answered, "I am here, in your heart."

For the first time, the Church New Year began in the Bronnitsa church without Father Ilarion's inspired serving of the moleben for the new academic year. Then, the first feasts of Venerable John of Rylsk (August 18/31 and October 19/November 1), Father's patron saint, took place without him. After that, there was the Feast of Venerable Ilarion the Great, Father's nameday, on October 21/ November 3. What magnificently festive, bounteous meals were held this day each year in Bronnitsa! Many guests were received, coming from all over to congratulate our dear father, to wish with all their hearts a golden crown for his angel, and for himself many long and blessed years in the Lord! For the first time, this day was celebrated without Father.

The next day was the Feast of the Kazan Icon of the Mother of God, which is especially revered in Bronnitsa, as it is throughout the region of Novgorod. "What a celebration that was at the Transfiguration of the Lord Church! For the first time this year, the joy of the feast was embittered by sorrow for our dear Father."

In January 2009, we began a new year of God's goodness. How jubilantly festive the Nativity and New Year holidays had been in Father Ilarion's time, with their invariable children's concerts at the church and in the school, attended by great numbers of people! With loving warmth, Anna Ivanovna Zhuravleva recalled the last Nativity children's concert: "How happy the children made Father and all of us, and how joyous Father was, with his face shining and a smile that never left his face … how the children greeted Father, and what touching things they said to him! It was impossible to remain dry-eyed."

Galina Petrovna Lashutina recalled our first Lent after Father Ilarion's repose:

> This year for the first time in over thirty years we are beginning
> Great Lent without Father Ilarion. But on Saturday of the 1st

week, the Bronnitsa parishioners shed streams of penitential tears
at the mere remembrance of his confessions each year on that day
(and then again on Great Thursday)....

I had known Father since 1964. For a great many years I
received guidance under Father's wing, grew accustomed to him,
clung to him heart and soul, and wanted to die with him. But I, a
sinner, must continue to work and pray.

Great Lent is beginning. For the first time our dear Father
will not send his congratulations, his charge, his fortification for
the Fast. I carefully keep all of Father Ilarion's letters, and now
I read many times over what he sent last year at the beginning of
the Holy Forty-day Fast, and I overflow with tears. I grumbled
considerably and was disobedient, but our dear father forgave
everything and pitied me. Now no one will pity me, or bring me
joy, or present me with a beautiful egg at Pascha. But I talk with
Father all the time, asking his advice and his blessing for everything, feeling with all my heart that God is with us! Father, our
dearly-beloved, unfading sunshine, is alive.

Without Father, we eagerly awaited the radiant day of Christ's
resurrection, in the hope that we unworthy ones may be vouchsafed
to meet him with deep faith in the coming resurrection unto life
eternal. How Father and all of us loved the days of the Holy Pascha
of the Lord, when for all of Bright Week, the church doors leading into the altar remain open—the beginning of the kingdom of
heaven on earth! Let us hear Father Ilarion's own voice, inflaming
the soul with grace-imbued paschal fire, drawing it into the heights
of heaven:

> "O Pascha great and sacred, Christ … !" Let us rejoice and be
> exceeding glad, for the Savior has brought perfect joy to earth for
> us. We hear of this joy in the Paschal hymns, and we sense it in our
> hearts, as they burn with love for the Lord.
>
> How is a sinful man not to rejoice, when in the Resurrection
> of his Savior a new world of holiness, truth, and blessedness has
> been opened to him, and he been given the chance to die to sin
> that he might rise and live with Christ? For the old man is cruci-
> fied with Him, and before the new man "the doors of paradise
> are opened.…" It is for this reason that in our Orthodox Church

there are no divine services so jubilantly joyous and festive as the Paschal services, nor any joy brighter and more full than our Paschal joy in the triumph of light over darkness and death, and in the transfiguration of our whole life into life incorrupt, into beauty immortal.

We simply must not fall into despair or remain despondent. Father Ilarion shed too many tears for us, too much blood and sweat; he put too much effort into the work of our salvation, that we might not be ashamed to stand before the face of the Omniscient, All-Good, Almighty One: "Take us, O Lord, for we are Thy servants...." Moving inexorably forward, time gradually closes the bleeding wounds, testifying that, although buried in the body, Father Ilarion does not leave us bereft of his protection even now, before the throne of God.

One such testimony is the dreams of various people following Father Ilarion's repose. Although the Church teaches that these are not to be believed, clergymen hold that certain dreams serve for the edification of believers. One of these is described here: "Three days after the burial I dreamed of a church. A great number of people are standing on the left and on the right. The doors of the church open, and Father comes into church. He walks along a green carpet spread down the center, looking straight ahead, neither old nor entirely young, about thirty years old, seeming gracefully sober, calm, and at the same time inwardly focused. The carpet begins rising smoothly up to the level of the solea, and Father ascends along it and enters the altar. Then the dream ends."

Father Ilarion's memory will forever be preserved in the Transfiguration of the Lord Church, which he restored, and in the hearts of his affectionately loved parishioners and spiritual children, who pray for him without ceasing. On holidays and weekdays, they come to his grave from near and far, and fall down to the mound of earth, talking with him as though he were alive, sharing both troubles and joys. They ask his blessing and beg for his prayerful intercession regarding their future paths in life, carefully preserving his image in their hearts, striving to live by his instructions, believing that his soul will stand before Him who holds in His hand the times and the seasons, and that his earthly service continues prayerfully in the eternal world.

Father Ilarion's grave is always adorned with live flowers; pannykhidas and litiyas are constantly served there, and the place exudes a special grace-imbued, comforting power. Those who live in other cities write asking after him and request liturgies and forty days' prayers for him in their own churches. One of Father's longtime spiritual children wrote, "One's soul constantly pulls towards Khutyn, where the grave of our dear father lies, to weep and sorrow that we did not take care of our treasure, and did not anticipate that this would happen."[1]

The following excerpts from other letters attest to the grief of those who loved him:

I want very much to go to his grave, to talk with our beloved Father, to cry, to tell him everything ... not a day goes by that I do not weep, and often I see Father in my sleep ... the dreams are not empty ones. Many want to come for Father's nameday ... now we meet with our dear, unforgettable Father once a year at his grave ... how unexpectedly his departure was for us, leaving us, his orphans; there are so many bright memories.[2]

My years passed like a dream. How sorry I am for Father! No words can express the sorrow. We used to swarm to our beloved Father like bees to a hive, and what joy and spiritual sweetness there was! Only tears now remain for comfort.[3]

Father, dear and beloved by all, we can't help missing you and shedding tears: no one will stroke us, or berate us lovingly; we did not think you would leave us orphans so soon.[4]

Some letters are quite radiant:

Father has gone, and it seems the whole world, the best that was in our lives, left with him. Yet at the same time the soul does not believe that this world remains only in the past: it senses it in the future, in eternity.[5]

Our dear Father's nameday is approaching, and we recall what joy there used to be: how people congratulated him, especially the children, how many touching and affectionate words were spoken, how many flowers and gifts ... words cannot express what spiritual celebration there was.... The smile of joyous gratitude never left Father's face.

Now our dear Father is not with us in body, but he is with us in spirit, and he knows everything and cares for everyone. Each of his spiritual children senses this. Father's prayers have become still stronger.... We want to come for Father's nameday, to gladden him and join with him spiritually in common prayer.[6]

What happiness that we had such a father, and that he will always, always be with us both here and there.[7]

Father Ilarion's moral strength calls us to keep sacred the memory of himself and of his spiritual asceticism, and with love to pass it on to a new generation of people.[8]

On this uplifting note, we repeat the words of comfort from the service book, which the hymnographer puts into Christ's mouth, followed by the response of the reposed: "Ye that have trod the narrow way of sorrow, all ye that in life have taken up the cross as a yoke, and have followed Me in faith, come, enjoy the honors and heavenly crowns which I have prepared for you.... Now I have reposed and found great rest, for I have departed from incorruption, and clung to life: O Lord, glory to Thee!"

An article was published to buoy the spirits of Father Ilarion's children, which included the following: "All who knew Father Ilarion personally, and those who have only heard tell of him from others who had the good fortune to receive guidance from the archimandrite—in a word, all of us have the opportunity to turn to the Lord in heartfelt prayer ... for the servant of God, who for many long years of his life offered up prayers for his 'little flock.'"[9]

Grant us, O Lord, a spirit of patience and courage to endure this separation, and may our hearts be touched by that holy, grace-imbued comfort which no separation or sorrow will be able to withstand. As for our Father, the greatest reward would be the Savior's words: "Those whom You gave Me I have kept; and none of them is lost."[10]

PART II

REMINISCENCES

CHAPTER II

Alive in Death
A Lofty Spiritual Image

ALIVE IN DEATH

Among Father Ilarion's papers, a typewritten manuscript was found, entitled "From the Works of Holy Hierarch Luke

> But the path of the just is like the shining sun, that shines ever brighter unto the perfect day.[1]

(Voino-Yasenetsky): There Is No Death!" The following is a condensed version of the text, as consolation to Father's orphaned children.

The entire world of living beings, even all nature, manifests the great law of gradual and endless perfection of forms, and it is impossible to suppose that the highest perfection achieved in earthly nature—man's spirituality—would not subsequently develop beyond the bounds of the earthly world....

The world has its origin in the love of God, and if people have been given the law "Be perfect, just as your Father in heaven is perfect," then they also must naturally be given the opportunity to fulfill this commandment, the opportunity for endless perfection of spirit. This requires the eternal, immortal existence of the spirit and an infinite variety of means for its perfection....

What is one to do? To what God has decreed we must submit.... Such is the common path of all.... The body dies, while the individual ... remains, and merely passes over to other orders of life.... We who remain weep for the departed, but their life is immediately eased: their state is the more pleasant....With the Lord there are no dead; all are alive with Him....

[The believer] is in a bright place, in a state full of comfort.... And every bit as alive as he was yesterday, on the eve of his death! Only then he was worse, and now he is better. That we cannot see him is no loss; he is still here. Our relations are as rapid as thought: they become even more intimate than they were here. For here space often separates us from our loved ones, but invisible existence narrows the distance, so that one has only to remember the deceased (in heartfelt, living memory), and already he is there.

What blessed peace wafts from these lines! What, then, is the meaning of our hearts' frequent pangs at the thought of death, and the involuntary sigh that escapes our breast: "All the same, how frightening it is to die...!" This is no wonder: all comfort pertains only to those who die in the Lord, and only those people die in the Lord who lived for the Lord and by the Lord's commandments here. Our bright, joyous faith tells us that the time will come when we will see our dear departed, and will live with them together, inseparably, eternally....

Here is what one of God's ministers, renowned archpriest Rodion Putyatin, says of this: "God, who is boundless love, will not separate those united by the bond of love."

Yes, whoever we love here on earth, whoever we share joy with here, we will rejoice with them there also. Our dear ones will then be even dearer to us, those close to our heart will be closer, and our mutual love will be still stronger. Knowing this truth, then, with what zeal and what readiness must we remember our deceased....

One can be distant from or close to the deceased. The stronger our love for the reposed, the stronger our prayer is for them, and the closer the deceased is to us. The prayer of faith can draw us so close to the deceased that we ourselves will sense the breath of their soul about us. It is primarily during prayer that heart communicates with heart.

Pray for the deceased (says Archpriest John of Kronstadt) as though your soul were in Hades, amid the flames, and you yourself were in torment. Feel their torment with your heart, and pray ever so ardently for their repose in a place of light, where there is neither sadness nor tears. "Pray one for another," the holy teaching tells us. And each day, and whenever you possibly can, repeat to yourself: "O Lord, have mercy on all those who stand before Thee this day!"[2]

On the page where these lines are written lies a piece of paper bearing writing in Father Ilarion's hand:

☦

For the departed:

"Pray for one another," Holy Scripture tells us.
    And each day, and whenever you possibly can, repeat to yourself:
"O Lord, have mercy on all those who appear before Thee this day!"

The text that follows, like the above excerpt which drew Father Ilarion's particular attention, testify to what an ardent intercessor he was for the departed. Each time he was at the liturgy, at the great and terrible sacred rite, he would commemorate the departed, and the departed would be vouchsafed to stand before the throne of God together with the angels and pray for their salvation, when the particles from the prosphora offered for them were submerged in the most-holy blood of the Son of God with the prayer: "Wash away, O Lord, the sins of those commemorated here by Thy Blood!" The hearts of the worshipers, sympathetic to the lot of friends and relatives beyond the grave, would overflow with profound gratitude to Father Ilarion for his good labor beyond all comparison for their sakes—lengthy, careful, never missing a single one of the names commemorated.

Let us also raise up our prayers for the repose of the soul of our beloved Father Ilarion, that it might sense that there are people praying for it, that there are still people on earth who love him, who believe that the eternally merciful Lord will hear us and will not leave our tearful sighs unheeded. "But the path of the just is like the shining sun, that shines ever brighter unto the perfect day."[3] "For though you might have ten thousand instructors in Christ, yet you do not have many fathers; for in Christ Jesus I have begotten you through the gospel."[4]

A LOFTY SPIRITUAL IMAGE

In 2009, Father would have celebrated thirty-five years of priesthood in Bronnitsa on October 18 and would have turned eighty-four years old on June 7. More than once on these anniversaries, he recalled the day when he first stood at the altar of God as a pastor, and of the sense of terrible responsibility before the human soul that he then felt. He often asked himself, Who are you? Why are you? What answer can you give before your flock for your long years of pastoral service? Such questions were heard from Father each year in his speech in response to the congratulations of the church's priests and parishioners. At the same time, however, he never drew any final conclusions. Rather, he could have repeated after the apostle, "Brethren, I do not count myself to have apprehended; but one thing I do, forgetting those things which are behind and reaching forward to those things which are ahead, I press toward the goal for the prize of the upward call of God in Christ Jesus."[5]

Naturally, our weak words and infirm spirit are incapable of depicting Father Ilarion's lofty spiritual image. Nevertheless, if we were to ask ourselves, What was Father like? Whom did we know him to be? The first answer that comes to mind is this: he was a great laborer in the field of Christian good works. He possessed an extraordinary work ethic and did more in a day than seemed conceivable to any of the people around him. Thy psychology of waiting passively was foreign to him. He was a laborer in the field of spiritual service to God and men and was never satisfied with the results of his accomplishments. He was constantly tormented by spiritual thirst for the quest for Christ and becoming one with Him.

The divine services, molebens, pannykhidas, baptisms, and weddings conducted through his cares and ministry are past counting: the sermons preached, advice and instruction given, apartments and houses blessed, the people buried in cemeteries, and those he helped both by word and deed to disentangle the tightly snarled knots of life. He always hurried and constantly reminded the people around him that they must make wise use of the time allotted,[6] which is already short,[7] and that all things may be restored except for time lost. He would quote from the Gospel: "I must work the works of Him who sent Me while it is day; the night is coming when no one can work."[8]

Above all, he called men to the acquisition of the Holy Spirit, to seek and obtain the kingdom of heaven and its truth. In all life's situations, Father Ilarion maintained a grace-imbued state of spirit, the fruits of which were love, joy, peace, long suffering, gentleness, goodness, faith, meekness,[9] and the other virtues that made it impossible to be near him and not feel glad just to be alive.

On the day after Father's repose, one of the female parishoners said, "Father left everything behind in complete order and splendor, enough to last to the end of time. Just cross yourself and pray, and save your soul!" Truly, in the time of his rectorship, Father Ilarion literally transfigured the Transfiguration of the Lord Church of Bronnitsa, both inside and out. He became for all a true focal point of Christian life. To this, the parishioners bear witness: "All our life existed first and foremost in and around the church. It became the harbor and calm haven of our hearts amid the storms and tempests of the sea of life, said one." Another said, "We would go into the church, and the powers of heavenly life would embrace us. The godless world with its vanity and passions was entirely forgotten, and one's soul was ready to embrace all mankind."

Father Ilarion constantly reminded people that the Lord manifests His special presence in the church, gazing upon all, and he would call all to stand with reverence before the face of God. He himself walked about the church quietly, in an orderly fashion. At times, it seemed that he was not walking at all, but floating, as though on a cloud. He always entered the church first and left it last. As Nadezhda Bulina of Veliky Novgorod recalled, "Father lived not for himself, but for the good of those around him, creating the most favorable atmosphere possible in the church." The Lord blessed all his good endeavors in the church.

Father Ilarion's outward appearance alone left an indelible impression: tall, stately, with long hair and a beard streaked with gray, and regular facial features. He presented a living revelation of spiritual life and was for us a source of faith and piety, love, compassion, and self-sacrifice. More than anything, he shone upon us by his simple, upright life, his ceaseless good works, and his living, active words. His face was radiant with a special inner light of righteousness and joy, and he wanted others to radiate this joy as well. With him, everyone felt upon themselves the breath of God. No books can begin to convey this feeling.

What was striking was how Father Ilarion's heart combined a constant contrite feeling of repentance with peacefulness and gladness of spirit, and a feeling, to quote the Holy and Righteous John of Kronstadt, "of extraordinary angelic and spiritual lightness of soul, soaring upon freedom of heart and thought," while the unsleeping foe mercilessly stung our own bowels, depriving our souls of peace and joy, inciting us to irritability, offenses, and condemnation. It is said that a person cannot inherit the kingdom of God unless he sees it in the face of another person. We who knew Father Ilarion have a glimmer of hope for salvation, for emanating from him we saw the radiance of eternal life.

Nearly always, he would begin by speaking sternly, with lowered eyebrows. "What did you come here for? Go back home; I already have millions like you!" was heard in the church repeatedly. Neophytes would drop their gaze and slump their shoulders in embarrassment, while the "old-timers" would exchange glances and smile. Upon seeing a person's humility, however, and observing his attentiveness and readiness to do as he was told, Father Ilarion would invariably conclude the audience with a smile, the dimples of which betrayed the good humor and kindness that the strictness concealed.

Both in questions of faith and in actual life, Father Ilarion was like a big child. He was distinguished by a remarkable childlike lack of malice, indicating his nobility and humble simplicity, which according to Saint John of the Ladder, is the sign of true repentance.[10] He combined grandeur and energy, quietness and rapidity of movement and action, forbearance and fire. It is impossible for words to convey the manly beauty of Father's countenance and his particular monastic spirit, so necessary for the living Christian soul.

Many of us have passed through the trial of Eastern philosophy and mysticism, of intellectual assimilation of divinely revealed truths, the danger of Pharisaical piety, and other complications. One did not need to explain anything at length to Father Ilarion. He would listen to you intently, hearing everything with his loving heart, and nod understandingly with bowed head. With each bow, a stone seemed to slide off your soul, and you breathed more freely and easily.

He never forced his authority on anyone and respected freedom of choice, thereby giving the individual opportunity for spiritual growth. Father Alexander Ranne noted the gift of eldership with which Father Ilarion was endowed. The Apostle Paul called this gift "the gift of wisdom and knowledge."[11] Father made all his decisions only as God directed. When approached for a blessing, he always inquired as to why the blessing was being asked. His blessing did not relieve one from responsibility for one's actions. When people attempted to ask a blessing for a matter they had already decided for themselves, he avoided giving it. He loved simplicity and clarity in both questions and answers.[12]

There was no pettiness or faultfinding in him. His nobleness, profound spiritual experience, and asceticism won him the profound love and respect of the people who flocked to him from all over, many of whom, after their first encounter with him, became his constant parishioners, and others his spiritual children. His simplicity and accessibility hid from those around him the full depth of his "inner man."

People became most acutely aware of this after he had departed into eternity. With pastoral wisdom and boundless suffering, he arranged the life of the church and the parish. Others mistook his patient and merciful treatment of them for spiritual weakness and thereby robbed themselves, not understanding that a righteous man is not subject to the rules of the law,[13] but rather himself becomes a law for others, a law embodied in himself. Such people did not understand that he based his actions not on the letter of the law, sometimes acting in direct opposition to it, but on love for his neighbor. Although they were shown every kindness by Father Ilarion, being confounded by the enemy's temptations, they judged him, tried to refute him, and undertook labors beyond their abilities to impress those around them. Yet, he bore ever upright the cross upon which their sins were crucified, remembering the weighty responsibility of the greater and senior to be the servant or slave of his juniors.[14]

CHAPTER 12

Worship, Prayer, and Fasting

CELEBRATING THE GREATNESS OF LITURGY

Father Ilarion experienced the greatest exaltation of spirit when serving the Divine Liturgy. He was always seized with a feeling of particular reverence and fear before the greatness of Him before whose altar he stood. He was a decisive advocate of the unity and integrity of the Russian Orthodox Church, personifying unwavering loyalty to her canons and dogmas and standing firmly in the truth. A strict adherent of the church typicon, he did not abbreviate the services; on the contrary, he always added something to them, striving to convey at least a small part of what he himself had experienced.

From his very first years of standing before the altar of God, at a time when overt preaching was prohibited, the divine services were the sole accessible means for the faithful to comprehend the Gospel, and Father Ilarion experienced each one as a feast. As Irina Vladimirovna Smirnova recalled,

> How Father loved the services in the church...! He would run, not walk, to church. In the morning he always arrived very early, around seven [o'clock]. First he would go about the church, checking everything, and then he would enter the altar, where he would serve the proskomide. Sometimes he would read several kathismata from the Psalter, or several akathists—Father understood everything. He had a handwritten commemoration book and a cover from an ordinary notebook, in which he kept a great many commemoration sheets. Sometimes he would ask

me to rewrite commemoration sheets that had become badly tattered. While rewriting them, at first I would smile frequently, as I encountered the notes Father had made, such as: "From Maria White Boots," or "From Galina the Nose." Later, however, I realized that this was how Father remembered the proprietors of the commemoration sheets, and that he was not simply mechanically reading through them: before his mental gaze there stood an image of a specific person that he held dear. And he kept these sheets for years, prayerfully commemorating all who turned to him.

If it was Father Ilarion's day to serve, he literally flew around the church. One minute he was praying inspiredly in the altar, the next he was singing on the kliros with the singers, and the next from the solea he was calling a parishioner over to say something that person needed to hear at that particular moment. Sometimes Father would leave the altar, go over to the railing on the solea, place his hands on it, and look out into the church at the worshippers. At such moments he resembled the captain of a ship, keeping a sharp eye on his crew and passengers to ensure that none perished in the depths of the raging sea.

Through Father Ilarion, the language of the services became more understandable, and we perceived the whole structure of church life as God's will for us. Our will and hearts were roused to meet this will, and we strove to keep God's commandments. As Galina Petrovna Lashutina remembered,

He served the vigil services in their entirety, and permitted no abbreviations. He knew all the services by heart, even the Lenten services, which are so very difficult. He was constantly with us on the kliros, praying in mind while simultaneously keeping a strict watch on what was sung and read. If you skipped something in your inexperience, he would immediately correct you. We thought he was so immersed in mental prayer that he would notice nothing, but such was not the case—he would correct us immediately. He perceived everything instantaneously, at the speed of sound. We just prayed and marveled. Over time, however, everyone came to understand what a gift Father possessed, and we ceased to be amazed.

Liturgically participating with Father Ilarion in the march of sacred history and its ontological and eschatological events—such as the creation of the world, man's fall into sin, and God's promises—at the Third Hour experiencing the gift of the Holy Spirit, at the Sixth the crucifixion of Christ, and at the Ninth the death of the Son of Man on the Cross, we not only prayerfully remembered past events but also became participants in the events of eternity. We became participants in that single liturgy that was once performed in the upper room in Zion at the Mystical Supper of Jesus Christ and His disciples. What we experienced personally spurred us to fundamentally change our lives and go the way of the cross of our Lord Jesus Christ, through whose death on the cross and resurrection, God's saving grace has been obtained for all men.[1] Before us, we saw and experienced "the whole life not of some great man, but of God, Who became incarnate, suffered, and died for us, who rose and ascended, and cometh again to judge the whole world."[2]

It is completely natural, therefore, that the deepest mark left in the souls of the Bronnitsa parishioners was that of the services of Great Lent and of the most festal of all festal services: the Paschal Liturgies. Never can we forget the hymns and readings of the Great Canon of Repentance of Saint Andrew of Crete during the Holy Forty-day Fast. Through Father Ilarion's voice, all the events of Old Testament and New Testament history, from the fall of our forefather Adam to the ascension of Christ, adhered themselves to the state of the sinful soul of each of those praying in church and shook it to the core. "I have put before Thee, my soul, Moses' account of the creation of the world, and after that all the recognized Scriptures that tell thee the story of the righteous and the wicked. But thou, my soul, hast followed the second of these, not the first, and hast sinned against God."[3] Frequently, Father's voice would break into weeping, and the whole church would weep with him.

Other stichera, however, exhorted and comforted, and at such moments, the soul was able to catch its breath: "I bring thee, O my soul, examples from the New Testament, to lead thee to compunction. Follow the example of the righteous, turn away from the sinful, and through prayers and fasting, through chastity and reverence, win back Christ's mercy."[4] As Father read it, the canon of repentance drew from the souls of its hearers a tremendously strong impulse toward repentance and moral correction. In no other church had the Bronnitsa parishioners experienced such feelings. At the Paschal Liturgy, Father would read the Gospel not only in Church Slavonic but also in Greek and Latin, as is done in several other churches, and which signifies that the joyous news of Christ's resurrection has gone forth "into all the earth,"[5] and that the risen Christ our God is now preached in all tongues.

Father Ilarion knew everything that went on in the church and in the souls of his parishioners. Many were puzzled as to how he could know everything about them. His secret was simple but hard to achieve, and beyond the abilities of most: Father prayed constantly, cleansing his soul with tearful repentance and prostrations, cutting off his own will, and enduring the many sorrows and sicknesses that he wore like chains. Hence, taught of the Holy Spirit[6] and guided by love for a given person, upon seeing that person for the first time, Father would delve into most of the hidden recesses of that person's soul and name his or her most secret sins. Father Ilarion knew better than you what you needed, what was harmful for you, and what was beneficial and salvific.

THE POWER OF INTERCESSORY PRAYER

As we know, a monk is an intercessor for the whole world. Father Ilarion was a great man of prayer and had the gift of the unceasing Jesus Prayer of the mind and heart, which burned in him like a perpetual lamp and illumined his whole countenance. Prayer was the source of his life, his spiritual breath, and one of his deeds of love and compassion for people—in the words of one Archimandrite, "a song of heaven once lost and paradise restored anew." So devoutly did Father Ilarion pray in the depths of his pain-filled heart for us proud and willful ones that one would have had to be a log or stone not to feel it. In offering the bloodless sacrifice on behalf of all and for all, he constantly reminded those present of the call of the apostle: "[P]ray without ceasing, in everything give thanks."[7]

At night also, he would maintain lengthy, prayerful vigils, sub-jugating his infirm flesh to his spirit, praying for all those suffer-ing and seeking prayerful consolation for himself from the King of Heaven, the Comforter of all who suffer. One of the women pari-shioners recalled, "In the church one always felt a conciliar spirit of prayer. When they sang 'I Believe,' one always thought: nowhere do they sing like that. We are grateful to the Lord that we had the good fortune to pray with Father at the divine services which he served."

"The prayer of a humble man," says the Word of God, "passes through the clouds."[8] Unceasing attentive prayer before the Lord made the heavenly Fatherland near and dear to Father Ilarion even while on earth. All asked his prayers, believing that they were effec-tive before God, and that God hearkened to them. Indeed, by his prayers, many received what they asked. As Anastasia Nikolaevna Baronova recalled,

> Once, while stoking the stove in the village, I got a splinter in my arm. It swelled up to the elbow, so that I could neither sleep nor do anything. My daughter called to ask how I was doing, and upon learning that I had not slept for four nights she scolded me roundly for not having told her earlier. She called Father, and asked him to pray. My arm was already as hard as a log. Suddenly, however, at two in the afternoon it began to release pus. For me this was an inexpressible miracle. I was and still am amazed by what happened, and at our Father's prayerful power. Forgive me, Father, the unworthy, disobedient, wayward, proud handmade of God Anastasia.

Maria Shevchenko of Veliky Novgorod recalled similar instances of healing through Father Ilarion's prayers:

> My brother Alexander suffered considerable back pain. He lay for six years, unable to move about, until I went to Father. "We'll pray for him," he said. Soon he was on his feet and had returned to work.
>
> When my mother became ill, her whole body hurt so badly that no one could touch her. She did not eat, and always stayed in bed. While caring for her I became like a skeleton myself—nothing

The Nativity of the Mother of God Men's Hermitage in Glinsk, 1958.

Spiritual mentors of the Glinsk Hermitage, circa 1950.

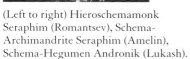

(Left to right) Hieroschemamonk Seraphim (Romantsev), Schema-Archimandrite Seraphim (Amelin), Schema-Hegumen Andronik (Lukash).

St Ilarion the Great, with whose name Ivan Fomich Prikhodko was tonsured a monk.

The icon of the Savior Not-Made-By-Human-Hands, which reminded the monks to moderate their speech.

The Glinsk monastery house, circa 1950. The right half contained the brothers' dormitory, and the left half was the monastery dispensary.

The Church of Holy Right-believing Prince Alexander Nevsky in Tbilisi, Georgia. Standing in the courtyard of the church in the early 1970s (left to right) are Archimandrite Modest (Gamov), Metropolitan Zinovy (Mazhuga), Schema-Archimandrite Seraphim (Romantsov), and Schema-Archimandrite Andronik (Lukash).

Hieromonk Ilarion studied at the Leningrad Theological Seminary from 1963 to 1967. Primarily an "A" student, as a fourth-year alumnus he was presented with the esteemed award of a pectoral cross by the Holy Synod.

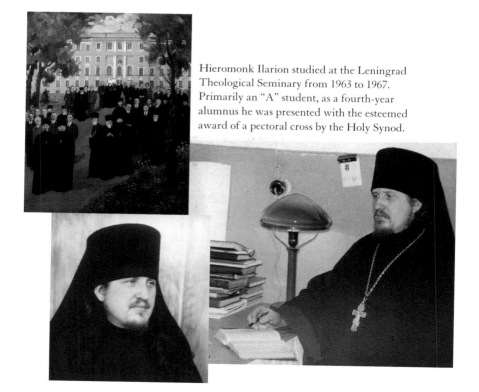

Father Ilarion graduated from the Seminary in 1967 (first row at left). He was then accepted into the Leningrad Theological Academy.

While studying at the Leningrad Theological Seminary, Father Ilarion also served as the dean of the Seminary church.

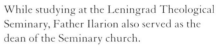

Father Ilarion proved to be a true spiritual treasure to the parishioners of the Church of the Holy Apostle Philip and to all the faithful of the Novgorod Region.

On October 6, 1975, Hieromonk Ilarion was appointed rector of the Transfiguration of the Lord Church in the village of Bronnitsa, Novgorod Region.

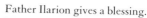

Father Ilarion gives a blessing.

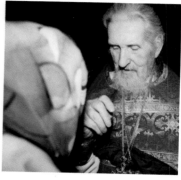

Father Ilarion reads the Gospel. Lighted candles are held by spiritual son Philip Wegh (right) and Sunday school pupil Maxim Konstantinov.

Truly, during the time of his rectorship Father Ilarion literally transfigured the Transfiguration of the Lord Church of Bronnitsa, both inside and out. He became for all a focal point of Christian life.

Archimandrite Ilarion with Hegumen Nikon.

At the walls of St Sophia Cathedral
in the Summer of 2007.

Father Ilarion venerates the relics of
the Holy Apostle Andrew (left) and the
relics of the Holy Venerable Martyr
Elizabeth Fedorovna in the Protection
Cathedral (below).

A special page in the spiritual chronicle of Father Ilarion's life is his blessed pilgrimage to the Holy Land during Holy Week of 1999. At left, he visits Mount Tabor.

Confession in the Iveron Monastery, Valdai, Novgorod Region, 2008.

Visitors came often to greet Father Ilarion. At right, he is joined by participants in the festal service in the village of Bronnitsa, 1996.

Father Ilarion's funeral at the Transfiguration of the Lord Church, May 29, 2008.

His Eminence Archbishop Luka of Konotop and Glukhov, Vicar of the Glinsk Hermitage (right), presides at the funeral service of Father Ilarion.

On the fortieth day after Father Ilarion's death, Archimandrites Antony and Sophrony came from the Glinsk Hermitage to pay respects.

but skin and bones. Father told me to pass on his blessing to her: "Endure your illness; arise and walk." At first mama did not understand, and argued with me, but then, in her faith, she got up and went to drink tea at the table. "Wait, Mama," I said; "let me help you"—but she was already sitting at the table. After Father's blessing and prayers Mama went wherever she needed on her own.

I thank you, O Lord! I am very, very grateful to Father for everything. His prayers saved both my brother and my mother. I myself once fell during Great Lent. For three years my shoulder hurt. I was healed at an unction service which Father served. He did much for all of us.

Anna Mikhailovna Gorlova also recalled a time of being healed through Father Ilarion's prayers:

Once I became seriously ill. Pneumonia. A temperature of 104°. Early in the morning I called an ambulance. The doctor immediately sent me to the hospital. In my half-conscious state I called Father, and told him that the doctor had pronounced my condition extremely grave, and had said that I might not return from the hospital. "There, there, don't imagine things. It's too early for you to die," said Father. "I will pray for you. Everything will be alright."

There was a flu epidemic at the time, and I was placed in the contagious isolation ward. I was constantly in delirium. The doctors fought for my life, and I pulled through the illness. My attending physician told me: "We didn't think there was any chance you would live. This is a miracle." Such was the power of Father's prayers and his love for men.

I recall how one woman came to Father with diabetes mellitus. Her medical statistics were off the charts, and the doctors had given her up for dead. In desperation she confessed long and contritely to Father, communed, and with tears asked for his prayers. When she returned to the church two weeks later, she fell to her knees before Father with tears, this time of profound gratitude: the illness had abated. A long gold chain from her neck hangs to this day in the case containing the Tikhvin Icon of the Mother of God.

The power of Father's prayers was felt by hundreds of people, who acknowledged that from their very first days at the Bronnitsa church, they felt as though a fortress had been erected about them, with walls reaching straight up to heaven. Vladimir Veselyev of Belgorod Region related how Father Ilarion's prayers brought the Lord's mercy to the Veselyev family:

> My son had undergone two operations at once, and was on the brink of death. I asked Father to pray for him, that the Lord would heal Dmitry. Later, M. Lena (now Mother Eufemia) related that Father had already seen Dmitry's place in heaven—a very beautiful one—but said: "His father will not be able to stand his son's death. We will pray to God." And by his holy prayers my son is alive to this day, working and raising his son with his wife, whom Father also obtained for them from God by his prayers.
>
> Four years after their marriage they still had had no children. In 2000 we all traveled to the train station in Belgorod to meet our dear Father. We asked his blessing. Father talked for a long time with my daughter-in-law and son, then remarked several times that they needed a "kinder" (Father loved to joke). Turning to my mother and signing us all with the cross, he said: "Paraskeva, you must pray that they have a child." Soon after, Evgenia conceived. When my grandson was born, the happy parents decided to name him in honor of their beloved Father, using Father's baptismal name—Vanechka. The boy now goes to school, and knows his prayers. In him I see, as it were, a continuation of our dear Father's life.

The family of Nadezhda Wegh of St Petersburg also received the Lord's mercy through Father Ilarion's prayers: "Once, after arriving in Jerusalem, my husband and I fell ill with asthmatic influenza. We returned with high temperatures (104°). In Petersburg no treatment was available for the Jerusalem flu. Night and day we were so choked up that it seemed we were about to depart this life. Then, at the most critical moment, when our last strength had failed us, Father suddenly called. 'I am praying, praying for you. Live! Live! Live!' It seemed as though we came out of hell, and by Father's prayers we recovered, when we had truly been on the brink of death."

Father almost never rested, as his cell attendant Valentina noted,

Father would get up at four. Prostrations. Then he would lie down, and get up again at six. Cell Rule of Five Hundred. Morning prayers. Midnight Office. Up to five canons to the Mother of God. Three akathists. Gospels and apostolic Epistles, which he would read until one in the afternoon. Breakfast after eleven. Rest. Compline. The service to the saint of the day. Canons to the Savior, five canons to the Mother of God, the canon of the day, and the canon to the Guardian Angel. Then he would take his tea. Evening prayers. He would go to sleep around eleven thirty or twelve. When he became weakened by illness, he abbreviated his rule somewhat: at first he prayed with his spiritual children, and then he began to pray alone.[9]

Ceaselessly continuing in prayerful vigils, subjugating his infirm flesh to his spirit, Father Ilarion prayed for all those suffering and sought his own prayerful consolation from the King of Heaven, the Comforter of all who suffer.

Olga Mikhailova of Veliky Novgorod recounted how she had been able to work through trying periods in her life through Father's ongoing comfort and blessing:

While he was alive, Father always took an interest in the results of matters for which his spiritual children asked a blessing. For instance, in the spring of 2008 I myself began certain necessary construction and repair work at my summer house. Subsequently, however, the cost of materials proved considerably greater than had originally been assumed. I was obliged to borrow money, and was considering a loan from the bank. When I had first asked Father's blessing he asked whether such expenses were within my means. At the time I didn't have a definite answer, since I had no experience in such affairs, but neither was there anyone to whom to delegate the matter. Some time later (not long before his repose) Father Ilarion asked about my affairs, and whether I needed help, to which I gratefully responded that so far I was managing. After Father's departure from this earthly life, however, I encountered financial difficulties. After a pannykhida I knelt before his grave and addressed him in thought: "Father, if you were alive, you would help me as you promised. Now I don't know how to get myself out of this. I've even spent the money I was saving for a trip to the Holy Land." And what do you think?! The next day a company executive of my acquaintance came to see me, whom I had helped to arrange a certain large-scale affair the year before. He had been unable to pay me at the time, and we agreed that they would pay me someday once their ship came in. He now paid me a substantial sum of money, with which I was able to complete my repairs at the summer house, leaving a sum to make the pilgrimage of which every Christian dreams. As I accepted the money, I suddenly remembered Father, and could barely hold back my tears.

Even when Father was alive, when I encountered financial difficulties I would ask him in simplicity of heart: "Father, pray that the Lord sends me additional work." And help always came! Once I was entrusted with a job that I had not the authority to refuse. The work, however, was obviously beyond my professional abilities, and the deadline was very tight. Father promised to pray. To my amazement, I completed the job on time, and even received a bonus. I was amazed, while Father, for his part, was so happy for me that my joy became inexplicably bright and replete.

Father was a very kind and caring pastor. His departure to eternity did not leave us orphaned. With the Lord all are alive! Hence, our dear Fr Ilarion hears our tears and cries, and prays unceasingly for our salvation with still greater boldness, since to him the mysteries of eternity are accessible! May his memory be eternal!

THE PLACE OF FASTING AND ABSTINENCE

He was a strict faster. Let us listen once again to one who was a constant witness to Father's vigils, his cell attendant Valentina: "The first week of Great Lent Father did not eat until Wednesday. On Wednesday he ate croutons and drank water. On Thursday he did not eat. On Friday he ate boiled potato and cucumbers. During Holy Week he did not take food until Holy and Great Thursday, when he communed of the Holy Mysteries. On Thursday he ate his food with oil, after which he ate nothing until the Holy Resurrection."

Mother Galina Slukina recounted a fasting lesson that she learned from Father Ilarion:

> One incident in particular stands out in my memory. We had had a baby, and I was breastfeeding. It was Great Lent at the time, and I came to Communion. Since I was feeding the baby, I had drunk milk and felt no compunction about breaking the fast. Without any sense of remorse I came boldly to confession and told of my actions. Father very sharply and indignantly told me that one must not break the fast, and that I was again trying to prove to him that I had every right to do so. Only when I clearly understood did he again speak to me in a warm, caring, fatherly way. For the rest of my life I never forgot that lesson.

CHAPTER 13

A Shepherd and Minister to His Flock

SHEPHERDING HIS CHILDREN

While standing internally before the throne of God, never for a moment did Father Ilarion forget those whom he served, who had to be preserved in peace, concord, and love. He helped reconcile quarrelling, subdue the disobedient, and quench feelings of jealousy and envy—"that hidden serpent"[1]—by rousing all to Christian zeal. Time and again, one would hear, "Father, bless...," and "Father, tell me...."

To one person, asking a blessing to get a divorce, he replied, "Why would you ever want that? Look over there (pointing to a corner where the unmarried women were standing). Those are the 'generals,' each her own mistress. But you, since you're married to your husband, bear your cross to the end." He would advise people to endure domestic sorrows patiently and pray to the Mother of God with faith that everything would someday change for the better. Father Ilarion loved to repeat, "God established family life, and it's not for me to annul it."

In contrast, another young couple somewhat past their prime asked his blessing to marry, but Father Ilarion foresaw that the marriage was not pleasing to God and did not bless it. The young couple, however, did not obey. They were registered and married, but a short time later were divorced. The marriage gained them nothing but grief. This is but one example of many such instances.

An elderly woman who came frequently from Novgorod to see Father Ilarion. Each time, he approached her with the same questions: "So you've been going around to various priests again? And what good will that do you? When are you and your husband going to have a church marriage?"

He had something to say to everyone. "Ivan," he yelled in an old man's ear, "when was the last time you were in church? You probably don't even remember! Do you smoke? Or drink? Or swear? Go to church, go more often, confess, commune. Ah, ah, ah ... You're done for, I tell you," yelling even louder into his ear, "if you don't start climbing down off the stove and going to church."

"And you," poking a woman in the ribs, who started at his attention, "Manya, or whatever your name is, I'll bet you're not keeping the fast! Just look how beet-red your cheeks are! Tsk-tsk-tsk ... so that's what you're up to during Great Lent! Fast, fast; save your soul by prayer and fasting."

"And you," shouting into a deaf man's ear, "do you still swear and beat your old lady? Say, 'I'll be good, I won't do it again; I'll stop swearing and fighting.'"

To another, he might say, "Well, well, look who's here. Where've you been traipsing about? You go a year without poking your nose into church. Promise me: 'I'll go to church, I'll pray, I'll make confession....'"

People left Father with a different inner disposition from when they came. Father Ilarion comforted and resurrected them to new life, since he understood everything through his own experiences amid labors to dispose his soul in accordance with his constant prayerful state before God. Galina Aleksandrovna Moskvina of the city of Severodvinsk was comforted by Father Ilarion through difficult periods in her life.

"My mother left me at the train station in Vologda when I was four years old. She took me from the children's home when I turned thirteen. She took me to my aunt's, her younger sister's, and I lived with her for a year, then for a year with my father, and then at fifteen years old I went to work at a military base.

"In 1963 I married, and in 1967 at my mother's request I left with the baby and came to stay with her in the city of Pechora, where my father had purchased a small house and she had been given a room. I arrived at my mother's in May, and in June, Father arrived from Leningrad, on vacation from the Academy. Thus, I became acquainted with our dear and beloved Father. When I approached him for a blessing, he said: 'Well, well, so another sheep has joined our flock.' Before meeting Father I had been a nonbeliever: I went to church with my mother, but had no faith. After conversing with Father, however, my eyes and heart seemed to open. Father placed love for the Lord God in my heart. Since that time I became a believer.

"My mother and I didn't get along, and in the end she turned us out of the house when my son was four years old. We went to stay with friends of mine in Petrozavodsk. While we had money they kept us, but the money ran out and we were politely asked to leave. In a strange city, homeless, unemployed, and with an infant in arms—it was horrible. But the Lord never abandoned me. Kind people helped me to find work and lodging. We lived with an old lady in her apartment. It happened that just before Christ's Pascha I hadn't a kopeck to my name—everything had gone to pay for lodging and child care. Then, the Saturday before Pascha, I received two notes: one for a package, and the other for 25 rubles (in 1968 that was a lot of money). When we opened the package, it was full of wormy croutons. The package was from my mother, and the 25 rubles—from our dear Father. To this day I cannot understand how Father learned our address. I had written to no one but a friend of mine, and that friend talked to no one; she had a different spiritual father, and my mother didn't like her. This was Father's first miracle for me.

"In difficult situations I always received help from him. Within half a year my mother came to Petrozavodsk, and begged us tearfully on her knees to come to her, saying that she had been wrong and would not quarrel with me any more. We went to stay with her, but our peace was short-lived. The money I earned I gave to her. Once I asked her for a ruble to buy a bucket of apples from a friend. She would not give it to me, and from that time on I began giving her money for the apartment, but buying all the groceries myself. My mother went and told Father of this. He summoned us both, and we knelt before him. My mother began to complain to Father that I was not giving her money and not feeding her. I was so offended at her saying such untruths before the icons and before Father that I burst into tears, got up, and ran from the room towards the door. Father said calmly: 'Galina, come back and kneel.' I obeyed, and Father then said: 'I see right through you, and I believe you.' That's what our dear Father was like. I forgave my mother everything, and I pray to God that she may forgive me everything as well, and that He may forgive us both."

MINISTERING TO HIS FLOCK

Father's flock grew greater by the year. As Mother Valentina (Bondarenko) recalled, people came to visit with Father not only from the surrounding settlements and villages, and the cities of Novgorod Region (Staraya Russa, Chudov, Valdai, Borovicha, Pestov), but also from other cities all over Russia, Ukraine, and Belarus. Below are many of Father's spiritual children who traveled great distances to visit with him:[2]

From suburban Moscow: Lyudmila, who moved to America, and Lyudmila, mother of Father Andronik

From Tver: sisters Vera, Nadezhda, and Valentina

From Moscow: friends of Vadim

From Severodvinsk: Galina Moskvina

From Arkhangelsk: Anna

From Pechora: Anna Ivanovna Zhuravleva, Peter Vlasov, Anna Gracheva, and Alexandra Mishchenko, who subsequently served as Father's cell attendant

From St Petersburg: Philip and Nadezhda Wegh, Evdokia Gorbunova, Maria Semenova, Natalya Mikhailovna Kuleshova, and Natalya Nikolaevna

From Yelets: Mother Tavifa, Nina and Valentina Kolyuzhnye, Elena Shcherbatykh, and others

From Bryansk: Vera Gashicheva (Nun Varvara), Alexandra Nozdracheva (Nun Anastasia), Tatiana Boikova, Klavdia Poddueva, Nina Igorevna, Tatiana, Valentina, Zinaida Sobolevskaya, Efrosinya Podolnaya, and many others

From Urengoi: Tatiana

From Khanty-Mansiysk: Raisa

From Stary Oskol: Mother Tatiana Emelianovna, Ekaterina Tarabanova, Mother Vera Prosvetova, Valentina Emelianova, Zinaida, Anastasia, and others

From the village of Borisovka: Maria and Valentina Bondarenko (the latter was Father's cell attendant), Mother Pelagea Mishchenko, Pelagea Marshuba, Antonina Bitsenko, Nina and Elena Kuchinskaya, Valentina Shishatskaya, and Alexandra Lutus

From Belarus: Fedor Sachkovsky, the Karlyukov family (Anna, Daniil, Pavel, and Maria), Olga and Mikhail Peregud, Nikolai Kolesnikovich, Lyubov, Natalya, Peter, Lyudmila, Nadezhda and Maria Kisel, Nikolai and Anna Nikolaevna Krasovsky (the latter was father's cell attendant), Tatiana Diskovets, Lyubov Novorai, the Sychevich family (Vasily, Nina, Anna, and Varvara), Ganu Babitsevich, Maria Tishkovets, Anna, Olga, and Galina (from Orsha)

From Zaporozhya: Lyubov and Larissa Kuznetsova, Lydia Mukhina, Vera Lebedenko, Olga Bondarenko, Ekaterina, Lyudmila, Tatiana, Nadezhda Babenko (from Kharkov), Sencleticia, Feodora, and Maria

Father's spiritual children gathered in Bronnitsa in the greatest numbers during the days of the Nativity Fast, Great Lent, and the Nativity and paschal feasts. People made preparations for the pilgrimage in a festal spirit, but at the same time, they were concerned by the need to overcome poor health, the rigors of travel, and other hardships. They traveled heavily burdened, not only with suitcases filled with presents but also with loads of sins and wondered, How would Father Ilarion meet them? Could he possibly send them right back? No such thing ever occurred. Never did anyone leave Father without being granted the grace they sought or receiving the gift of both the Holy Spirit and their daily bread. The moleben for travelers was served, the parting blessing was given again and again, and at parting was heard, "Farewell! Forgive me, as I do you.

God willing, we shall meet again." Many also communicated with Father through telephone calls and letters, which all of the spiritual children under his pastoral care needed greatly, since all his counsels and exhortations were founded on humility and love. From these virtues, he produced all the rest: heartfelt contrition, repentance, meekness, patience, reserve in conversation, and the others.

Below are excerpts from two of Father Ilarion's letters to his long-distance spiritual children:

> I am deeply grateful for all your best wishes and regards. My little sister O., these words are for you. See to it that you don't go making friends with all sorts of boys: choose one for life who will be reliable, like your father, and never under any circumstances desert this task. Make sure that you do as I have written.

> Dear friends, I sincerely thank you for your letters, but I wish to bring to your attention that you should not worry about being unable to send me money. I have plenty of everything, and you are paying off debts which you are in up to your neck.... I will write to you and pray for you, and you will always be with me.

Everything that came out of Father's mouth was founded on the Holy Scriptures and the works of the Holy Fathers. His advice and exhortations were not theoretical reasoning but knowledge of the soul gained by experience. He taught what he himself lived and followed. He left no one's petitions unheeded, responding to all with love.

The guests departed, while we, "the fledglings of Ilarion's nest," warmed by his vigilant daily care for us, for the thousandth time realized our good fortune all over again. Our hearts overflowed with gratitude to God for His mercy in allowing us to be with Father Ilarion, hearing his voice in the mornings saying something along the lines of, "God's blessings on you. What's the matter, asleep on your feet?" or, "Listen, we have some papers that need to be filled out, and how are we to do that ... any idea?" (Here, Father would begin singing some merry tune from his younger days.) The answer would come as usual: "Oh, don't worry, Father, it'll be alright. You do what you have to do. We'll fill them out." Unless the child slipped up, the conversation nearly always ended just as merrily: "God bless you. Don't sneeze, don't cough ... our greatest respects to you."

PRACTICING OBEDIENCES

Knowing that every good work begins with obedience and patience, following in the footsteps of the Glinsk elders, Father set "obedience higher than prayer and fasting,"[3] and considered it "the wages of eternal good things."[4] He maintained unquestioning obedience to the Glinsk elders and subsequently preserved holy obedience to his own Father Ioann (Krestyankin), remembering the testament of Father Seraphim (Romantsov): "For even Christ, when He came to earth, chose not the life of a hermit or a stylite, but the form and rule of subjection to the Heavenly Father.... Being in subjection, rejoice that you also abide in the likeness of our Lord Jesus Christ.... Can anything be more blessed?!"[5] According to the elders, nothing is more blessed than fulfillment of this most important Christian virtue, but neither, apparently, is anything more difficult in the life of a Christian. This is particularly true of the young person of today, who sets self-will above obedience, vain thinking above humility, and his or her own proud mind above the will of God, and hence endures oppression and sorrow in soul.

As has already been noted, Father Ilarion never forced the authority of his eldership on anyone. Rather, he knew how to approach a person so that all who voluntarily chose him as their spiritual guide would fulfill God's will for them of which he was the conductor, at first with difficulty, then with joy, and would gradually learn to heed the voice of their conscience, that is, the voice of God in the depths of their souls. Father Ilarion's spirit seemed to live in and steer their souls. One such person under obedience was the nun Evdokia, now reposed in the Lord. Always meek, hard working, quiet, and welcoming, she was a servant to all and regarded herself as nothing, yet she left a bright trace in the souls of those who knew her. Another such person, according to the old-timers, was Father's cell attendant Anna Nikolaevna Krasovskaya. In everything, these spiritual children cut off their own will, committing themselves wholly to Father. They were prepared to carry out any obedience from him and responded instantaneously not only to his every word but also to his every glance, eye movement, and gesture.

He himself "learned obedience by the things which He suffered"[6] and strove in every way through obediences to bring those under obedience to him to salvation. If a person was obstinate, however, he would silently bow his head and look at the floor, a sign that there was nothing he could do to help. He sorrowed for the wayward and the disobedient and prayed for them, yet he continued to help them materially, of which they frequently took advantage.

"The kitchen and the bakery are the first school for testing beginners," we read in *The Glinsk Paterikon*.[7] In the kitchen, Mother Evdokia, Elena Ivanova, Ekaterina Dmitrieva, Svetlana Rychkova, Galina Baranova, Klavdia Zykina, Valentina Vasilyeva, and others successfully bore their obediences. The challenging task of baking prosphora was performed at various times by Valentina, Antonina, Raisa Zubkova, and Klavdia Nikitina.

Klavdia Nikolaevna loved her work and readily told of Saint Nicander, who was given the complex and difficult task of baking prosphora. Venerable Nicander fulfilled this obedience with joy, reasoning, "If our Lord Jesus Christ called the bread prepared for the Mystical Supper His Body, I ought to rejoice that God has vouchsafed me to prepare such loaves, upon which the great and terrible Mystery is performed: in a manner wondrous and incomprehensible they are transformed into the Holy Body of Christ."

Anna Mikhailovna Gorlova, Galina Petrovna Lashutina, Valentina Sirotkina, and Valentina Novikova had long served as readers in the church, but after a time, some of the novices took up this task. Of the young people, the Pavlina Audinova, an alumna of the Sunday school, and the novice Irina Vladimirovna Smirnova read particularly well and distinctly. Father Ilarion would give some of the novices something to copy from the letters and diaries of the Holy Fathers. In later years, this was primarily the task of Irina Vladimirovna Smirnova. According to *The Glinsk Paterikon*, these ready-made spiritual excerpts were inserted following a salutation to a given addressee, and the letter was complete. No one who was expecting a response and advice was ever disappointed. This form of letter writing was the practice of some of the Glinsk elders, such as Father Seraphim (Romantsov).

Some, even those without a good ear or voice, sang in the choir. Father Ilarion felt that their modest participation in the hymns was beneficial for the health of their souls. He never gave obediences beyond a person's strength, appointing each according to the measure of his or her strength, skills, and abilities. There were many different kinds of obediences, such as cleaning the church vessels, washing, ironing church vestments, sweeping the church floor, chopping wood, stacking bricks, digging, weeding the garden, planting and watering vegetables, bringing in the harvest, and tending the flowers.

Irina Vladimirovna Smirnova remembered instances of performing such obediences under Father's instruction:

> At the Bronnitsa church, on the territory in front of the church, in the garden, and even on the shore of the river near the church—everywhere cleanliness and order reigned. Much of Father's efforts and health went into this. More than once I participated in obediences involving cleaning up and repairing the church, moving wood to the shed, working in the garden, planting trees, etc. "You're all Soviets—pioneers, octoberkins," Father would tell us. But he wanted to make us into Christians, and taught us to work constantly. I recall one very telling incident. One spring day we ploughed a field and planted it with potatoes. When Father went to check our work after we had finished, he suddenly spied a small patch of ground that had gone unploughed (apparently it had been difficult for the horse to reach). Pointing to the patch, Father exclaimed: "So it's just going to loaf around on me, is it?" The ground was promptly ploughed and planted with potatoes. Nothing and no one loafed around on Father.
>
> Being himself a great laborer, he taught us also to labor, frequently in ways that were completely unexpected. I recall one such episode that involved painting the inside of the church. Father had given me and one other handmaid of God the obedience of painting stars on the ceiling near the entrance to the church, since the previous ones, the work of a professional artist, had been painted

over. I had always gotten straight Cs in art at school, but the obedience had to be fulfilled. We climbed up to the top of the scaffolding, where we found no railing around the edges. Our hands and feet shook; we were afraid to stand up all the way, and we were looking down at the stone floor the whole time. One way or another we painted a few small stars; then, soaked from the strain, we climbed down. At that moment Father came into the church. "What, are you going to be painting for me all week?!" In a flash we flew back up the scaffolding, and standing up straight we began quickly painting stars. In this way, through the thorns to the stars, by our dear Father's prayers we made it through each time. No matter how difficult and unfamiliar the work that we had to do, we believed that by Father's prayers it would all be done.

Especially active in physical labor were Nun Evdokia, Constantine Sergeev, the novice Lydia Arefyeva, Maria, Maria Esina, Lydia Zorina, Svetlana Mikhailova, Svetlana Rychkova, Valentina Vasilyeva, and many others. In the last two or three years of Father Ilarion's life, Sergei Tarasov, Alexei Polikarpov, and Vladimir Fedorov helped considerably around the property. Various construction jobs were done by Nikolai Ivanovich Fedorov, Vadim Simon, and Gennady Ivanov.

For more than thirty years, the choir was directed by Lyudmila Nikolaevna Sirota, who had gathered an excellent group of chanters. Of these, the voices of Boris Ivanovich Pogudin and Alexander Semenovich Larin stood out in particular. The faithful servants of this sacred art during Father Ilarion's time of service were Irina Nikolaevna Nefedova, Elena Kuzmina, Ekaterina Titenko, Nadezhda Bulina, and others. The Bronnitsa choir always sang solemnly and harmoniously. As Father Andrei (Poltoratsky) said, there was something special about it, something intangible, that other choirs lacked. Father Ilarion loved to sing, and when he did, it seemed that his heart and mind were one.

The greatest workload, naturally, lay on the shoulders of Father's cell attendants, Mothers Valentina and Alexandra. Mother Valentina had the closest spiritual relationship with him. She enjoyed his particular respect and trust. In the last two years, however, due to her elderly mother's illness, she was obliged to return frequently to her homeland, and Mother Alexandra bore the full weight of labors that were beyond others' endurance. Both mothers had the opportunity to see some of Father Ilarion's particular ascetic labors and works, and hear him tell of grace-imbued revelations which he had been vouchsafed, and which he did not permit them to relate to others.

MERCY AND COMPASSION

When doing good, Father Ilarion never expected good in return and taught others to do the same, for "what credit is that to you?"[8] Despite what many perceived as excessive strictness, his spiritual children saw him first and foremost as compassionate both to the good and to the ungrateful and evil.[9] He constantly reminded his flock to give alms not in men's sight but in secret, to pray and fast, and to forgive one another.[10] He would forgive a repentant person on the instant and accepted not only the laborers of the first hour but also of the eleventh, who as in the Gospel parable were hired at the end of the workday, that is, turned to God late in life, yet through His love and mercy, received their reward together with the first who had persevered in labor.

Father Ilarion was extremely demanding of himself and ascribed anything done well to God. Like a faithful warrior of Christ, he was guarded from praise and vainglory by his Orthodox belief in all the dogmas of the Ecumenical Church, bequeathed her by the holy apostles and the Holy Fathers, and assimilated by the Glinsk elders and, through them, by himself.

Father Ilarion taught his flock mercy, which of all ministries "is most akin to God."[11] The instances of his mercy toward people are countless. Anna Mikhailovna Gorlova recalled an instance of his mercy toward her:

> On the eve of Lent I became so sick that I could not even make a prostration in church. I became so sad. Aloud, looking at Father Ilarion's photograph, I said: "Father, take pity on me and pray for me." The night of Clean Monday I fell asleep, and toward morning, around six o'clock, I had a dream. I was in the church, on the

ambon. Beside me, in simple monastic garb, was Father (I was on his right). The icon of the Iveron Mother of God was hanging there. Father gave the tone, and began singing the troparion to the Iveron Icon of the Most-Holy Mother of God (commemorated on October 13/26, February 12/25, and the Tuesday of Bright Week). Father was singing some unfamiliar, seemingly unearthly chant, and his singing was somehow so moving and penetrating that as I started to sing along I began to sob in my sleep. I woke up sobbing. As I recall, as he sang he emphasized individual words (in italics):

"From Thy holy icon, O Lady Mother of God, *healings and cures* are bestowed abundantly upon those who run to it *with faith and love*. So also do thou visit my *infirmity* and have mercy on my *soul*, O good one, and *heal my body* by thy grace, O most-pure one."

Never have I met anyone who seemed to sense and pity each person as he did. He always had this trait, and it remains in him for all time. He always hastened to meet people, bringing help for soul, spirit, and body.

After "meeting" Father Ilarion in my dream I went to the church, and could not calm down until evening came. No sooner had I turned to him than he had immediately responded and lifted my spirits for some time to come. That is what Father Ilarion was like.

Here is yet another episode from the last year of Father's life. Father Andrian, whom Father Ilarion had known since his studies in the Leningrad Theological Academy and his time in Pechora, came to see him. Father Andrian had also visited him in Bryansk. He was a short, unkempt little man, and as he was walking, he got caught up in the mantle Father Ilarion had loaned him for the service. The mothers began laughing, but Father Ilarion scolded them roundly and threatened to lambaste them for such lack of regard for a priest.

Father Ilarion was greatly saddened by one very talented person, who would go off on long bouts of drunkenness. He prayed considerably, asking God that He not leave that person's unhappy soul to perish, and warned the man, "When I die there will be no one to pray for you."

CHAPTER 14

Sorrows and Consolation

THE YOKE OF SORROW

Being firm in his faith, Father could glory in the face of tribulations also.[1] In the vast experience of his spiritual life, his heart had known "both the easy yoke of the Savior and the heavy, unbearable yoke of Satan," and he had wrestled against "spiritual hosts of wickedness in the heavenly places."[2] We have merely heard of this in passing, and it is not for us to theorize upon. We will cite but one example from Paraskeva Veselyeva of Belgorod Region:

> Once we were with Father in Bryansk. We were sitting in the parlor with him and talking. Two people were cleaning in the hallway, where there was a large case with three shelves. They glanced at it, and there, on the third shelf, two demons were sitting in the form of cats, with light brown fur and large eyes. No cats that size exist. The people began to shoo them away, but the "cats" did not budge. The women ran in to us, saying: "Father, just look at those cats on the shelf! They won't leave!" He got up and took us with him. How frightened we all were! Father, however, went up to the "cats" and calmly said: "Why have you come here? Who invited you?" They just sat there, shifting from side to side, their wide eyes riveted on him. "Go on, get out of here!" Father ordered them. Then, to one of the women: "Just you hand me that club over there." He held out his hand. How those "cats" flew! Like lightning they were off the shelf and sprinting for the door (which was open and led to the garden). "And don't you ever let me catch you around here again!" Father called after them. The garden was

surrounded by a high wooden fence, which they scaled instantly. To us, Father said: "You see how powerless the demon is?"

Father Ilarion's impartiality, his spiritual guidance that constantly drew on the Glinsk elders, and his firm stance in spirit and in truth in times when the mere mention of God or the Church was interpreted by the authorities as little less than treason and provoked irritation, misunderstanding, and opposition. Moreover, jealousy of Father, resentment of him, and later, physical infirmities, illnesses, and lengthy services to the point of complete exhaustion—when he had to take pills by the handful and, after the regular services, still serve the various services of need, such as baptisms, weddings, and pannykhidas—at times brought him to the point of complete collapse.

In addition to these labors and sorrows, Father Ilarion had to contend with his own hot-blooded nature. At times, zeal for the salvation of his neighbors gained the upper hand over love and understanding of their infirmities, and then many took offense, never imagining what spiritual efforts he made on their behalf, how many tears he shed to incline God's mercy toward a sinner, and how many prostrations he made on his or her behalf.[3]

According to Gennady Ivanov, an altar server and the church watchman from the village of Proletary, "Father's fear of God, which never left him, and his indiscriminate love for people caused him to worry greatly on account of his obligatory strictness with his parishioners and spiritual children, to sorrow in their sorrows, and to grieve in their infirmities. But how he rejoiced at even the most seemingly insignificant of our successes!"[4]

Despite Father Ilarion's outward quick temper, he nevertheless possessed the most profound humility. Frequently in his sermons or in listing sins at confession, he would primarily blame himself for the sins named and ask forgiveness if he had offended anyone in any way. If he saw that a person had been wounded by his reprimand or was in tears, he would invariably ask for forgiveness. Father Ilarion might even kneel before the person or dispel his or her despondency in a flash by a kind, lighthearted joke. Even a minute's conversation with him concentrated a person's thoughts on the spiritual and helped resolve his or her sins. Anyone who was accustomed to see himself or herself as virtuous was humbled after seeing Father's distress over his or her troubles and prayers for the forgiveness of his or her sins.

Mother Galina Slukina noted this distress in Father:

> Father was always very distressed if he accidentally offended anyone, and always sincerely asked forgiveness, age and status notwithstanding. Once, during the All-Night Vigil, he reprimanded me in a rather sharp tone of voice. In the morning I came into the church while he was censing. As he passed me, he said imploringly: "Don't be angry with me; I'm serving the Liturgy, you see.... Forgive me."
>
> One would think everything would have been long forgotten. Two months later, however, Father was preparing to leave on vacation. I was stacking wood in the shed when he approached me, holding out some chocolates, and again began to urge me to forgive him: "Don't just forgive me; forgive me from your heart...." Thus he humbly taught us to correct our mistakes, and to fear remaining unforgiven.

Father's monastic path was that kind of labor for Christ's sake that is accessible, in the words of a contemporary hieromonk, "to but a few, removed from society for its survival." Father Ilarion frequently quoted the words of one monk: "If people in the world knew all the joys and consolations of soul that a monk experiences, there would be no one left in the world: everyone would become monks. But if people in the world knew beforehand the sorrows and torments that are visited upon a monk, no flesh would ever dare take the monastic rank. No mortal would have the resolve."

If we look at the trials that fell to Father Ilarion's lot from the standpoint of the mystery of human suffering, it is difficult to suppose that he, robed in the Lord's might and selflessly serving God and men, did not endure the sorrowful illnesses and other burdens of earthly monastic life. In answer to our sympathy for him, he could have responded in the words of Venerable Nektary of Optina: "I am doing poorly, but grace is doing well."

Several times in his sermons, Father Ilarion told the story of a certain Egyptian father who once beheld a spiritual vision. We relate it here as recounted by Saint Ignatius (Brianchaninov):

> Three monks, he saw, were standing on the seashore. From the opposite shore came a voice: "Take wings, and come to Me." Following this voice, two monks received fiery wings and swiftly flew across to the opposite shore. The third remained where he was before. He began to weep and to wail. At last he, too, was given wings, but weak ones, not fiery, and he flew across the sea with considerable difficulty and effort. Often he grew weak and began to sink into the sea. Seeing himself sinking, he would begin to wail pitifully, and would rise a little way above the sea and fly on, low and slowly. Again he would weaken, again he would descend into the deep, again he would cry out, again he would rise up a little way; and he barely completed his flight across the sea, utterly exhausted.
>
> The first two monks depicted the monasticism of early times, while the monasticism of latter times, meager both in numbers and in prosperity, was depicted by the third. The holy fathers of a certain Egyptian skete once prophetically discussed the latter. "What have we done?" they asked. One of them, the great Abba Ischyrion, replied: "We have fulfilled God's commandments." "What shall they do who come after us?" they asked him. The Abba replied: "They shall receive [will perform] half the work that we have." Again they asked him: "And what shall they do who come after them?" Abba Ischyrion replied: "They will no longer perform monastic work, but tribulations will be visited upon them, and those that withstand shall be greater than we and our fathers."

When drawing near to serve the Lord, Father Ilarion prepared his soul for temptation.[5] He ascended the ladder of sorrow without a murmur, considering himself worthy of still greater punishment, and he taught others to bear their life's crosses uncomplainingly and recognize God's will for them in this. He frequently repeated the last words of the Holy Hierarch John Chrysostom: "Glory to God for all things." There was also a song about Elder Seraphim of Sarov that he liked very much, with the refrain:

Glory to God for all things,

Glory to God for all things,

Glory to God for both sorrow and joy.

He loved this song as it was performed by the children of the Sunday school, and he used to sing along with them.

He could have repeated the words of Job the Long-Suffering: "Shall we indeed accept good from God, and shall we not accept adversity?... As it seemd good to the Lord, so also it came to pass. Blessed be the name of the Lord."[6] Hence, the yoke of sorrows for him was easy. The evil from those who abused him, always thinking themselves in the right, he always bore as his own. He worried about the person, persuaded, exhorted, prayed, gave presents, and constantly removed particles from the prosphoron for him or her at the proskomide.

Looking at Father and listening to his sermons about the much-suffering righteous ones and the words he often quoted about how the Son of Man found no place to lay His head, we were ashamed of our own sadnesses. Such references would instantly dispel our unwholesome self-pity. With him, grief seemed of no consequence. No one ever saw him sad, and he conversed with everyone with childlike trust. If anyone spoke ill of another, he promptly cut the condemner off: "What do Vanka, Manka, Petka, and Svetka matter to you? Look to yourself." Or, he would resolve the situation on the spot in the presence of both accuser and accused: "Listen here, she says that you did such-and-such. Is that true or not?"[7] Investigations like this left you with no desire to tell him anything bad about others, and you began to seek the source of the problem in yourself. Rebuking someone with good intent, however, out of love for God and for that person, without defaming the person's name and dignity, was not something that Father Ilarion considered a sin.

According to *The Glinsk Paterikon*, "Holy Scripture gives two instructions: 'Reprove' and 'do not reprove.' The first commands, the second forbids. *Reprove not a scorner, lest he hate thee* (Prov 9:8), for a sinner finds reproofs unpleasant, since reproofs wound the ungodly man. The Word of God says: reprove. Whom? Reprove a wise man, that you might be the wiser. What, then, does this profit? It profits in that he himself will be corrected and will truly love thee."[8] The closer a person was to Father Ilarion, the more he or she would be chastised. Yet, the person rebuked would receive this strictness with love and gratitude.

Father Ilarion covered all unkindness toward himself with love. Among his papers, several crumpled pages were found that testified to the manifestations of his great love for all, and to his penitential spirit. Mother Valentina said that she once caught a glimpse of these papers, but Father hid them and would not let her examine them. On them, scribbled in pencil, were notes of how many prostrations he had made throughout the year and during the Holy Forty-day Fast, how many canons he had read, and how much of the holy Psalter. The following are examples from his notes: "By my nameday, that is, by October 21, 1979, or November 3, 17 thousand 600 prostrations were made. In one week, that is, in six days from 11/XI to 17/XI, 1979 (from Monday to Saturday), 5,300 (five thousand three hundred) prostrations were made. By the Nativity Fast—27 thousand. Total by 24/XII, 1979—47 thousand…. In the course of the Nativity Fast, 29,960; during Holy Lent, 60,900…. Great Lent of '81—268 thousand prostrations…. Holy Psalter read 22 times during Great Lent, 2005…. Canons to the Mother of God read approximately 200–252 times per year." There is also a note specifying that "the necessary number of prostrations has been made through the year 2025."

These records were not intended for others' eyes, and we have cited a few examples merely to clearly demonstrate what a price Father Ilarion paid for our sins. He endured spiritual struggle because of the invisible foes that assailed him, enduring the wounds they inflicted on his soul, repelling them by prayers, by constantly calling on the name of Jesus Christ, and by prostrations, repentance, and communing of the Holy Mysteries of Christ. He never forgot the commandment of the Glinsk elders: "Drink reproach like water."

One of Father Ilarion's notebooks contains the following note as part of his materials for a sermon:

By God's will, our earthly human life from cradle to the grave is filled with many sorrows. These sorrows, however, have a beneficent value for us. They show us the path to salvation and lead us to the Heavenly Kingdom. Hence, we must patiently endure our sorrows and have unshakable faith in God's mercy. We must endure sorrows and sicknesses with meekness and submissiveness to God's will, that through them our souls might be cleansed of sins and learn true love, which *suffereth long*.

The Lord, in taking upon Himself the sins of the world, did not take His enjoyment in a happy life on earth, but endured and bore the great Cross of sorrows from the manger to Golgotha. Instead of *the joy that was set before Him*, Christ the Savior *endured the cross, despising the shame, and is set down at the right hand of the throne of God* (Heb. 12:2).

The Holy Hierarch Gregory the Theologian tells us: "I gaze upon Christ in gladness even when He sends me sorrows; I rejoice that sadnesses make me lighter, like gold that had been mingled with dust and is now cleansed."

In one of Father's notebooks, the following poem was found, which expresses well his attitude toward sorrows:

Whoever once takes up his cross,

Ever crucified is he,

And if happiness exist

Eternally happy will he be.

No prize is there for deeds well done;

Love and sorrow both are one.

But greater than all goods, and dearer,

Is this sorrow to its bearer.[9]

WONDER-WORKING ICONS

It is clearly no accident that Father Ilarion's icon of the Sorrowing Mother of God from Jerusalem was the first to begin streaming myrrh. After it, many other icons in his cell also began to stream myrrh. As Nun Valentina recalled, "There was another icon, one highly venerated by Father, of the Sorrowing Mother of God. It was kept at Mother Varvara's in Bryansk, and was already very old and completely darkened. When Father traveled to Bryansk in 2003, he took it and gave it to Alexander Grigoryevich Alentyev to be fitted with a new case. When the latter began dismantling the icon in Father's presence and removed the glass, on the glass they saw an image of the Mother of God identical to that on the icon. Both this icon and the glass were kept in Father's cell."

I saw how the icon grew lighter by the day. From beneath the soot, the faces began to brighten, and the garments to shine, of the Mother of God and the Pre-eternal Infant. First, above the outline of the face (all that could be seen of it) of the Most-Holy Mother of God, as though crowding it out, the renewed face began to show through with increasing clarity, and above the outline of the Divine Infant shown through His renewed face. By the feast, nearly the entire image had been renewed, and the icon had become sky blue.

It has been noted that the phenomenon of an icon's renewal has previously occurred at particularly tragic times in the history of Russian Orthodoxy. Numerous miraculous icon renewals took place immediately following the October Revolution of 1917. In the Novgorod Uezd in 1925, the authorities tallied over 150 such icons. These testimonies of God were summoning the people to profound repentance and cleansing, and reminding them of the Last Judgment. Is it not to this that the icons called, and continue to call, us sinners also through our Father Ilarion, reminding us that the image of this world is passed, that in the world we will be sorrowful, that wherever we may be we will never search out a place devoid of sorrow, and that we must bear the yoke of Christ in meekness and humility? For the Lord Himself said directly, "Take My yoke upon you and learn from Me, for I am gentle and lowly in heart, and you will find rest for your souls."[10]

ON THE WINGS OF FAITH AND LOVE

Father Ilarion was "all things to all men,"[11] simple and merciful. At the same time, one could imagine what high spiritual voltages were surging through him. In the works of Archimandrite Sophrony (Sakharov), we read, "on the outside monks may be likened to high-voltage power lines, upon which little birds may alight and sit safely, while through the wires energy is coursing that moves trains, lights homes, and provides heat. All life moves by its power alone."[12]

The blessed Elder Silouan had this to say of the monk: "This is a person who walks with his feet on the ground and works with his hands, and no one sees that in spirit he abides in the eternal God."[13] That Father Ilarion abode constantly in the eternal God became increasingly obvious in the last days of his life. In so doing, he also simultaneously abode with and in his Christian brothers, sisters, sons, and daughters both near and far, without seeming to single anyone out as more deserving than another.

People learned much from Father Ilarion about how to live in a godly fashion. He helped them bear numerous crosses throughout their lives. Ignoring his own sicknesses and sorrows, everything was covered by love, which lent considerable power to his advice and exhortations. His strength of spirit was particularly astounding and enabled him to transform those whom he shepherded into sparks of divine fire.

Thus, through love for God and neighbor, Father achieved the goal of the ministry of a pastor of God: "To give wings to the soul, to tear it from the world, and give it to God; to preserve what is in His image, if it be whole; to support it, if it be threatened; to restore it, if it be damaged; to lodge Christ in the heart with the aid of the Spirit; and to deify those of the highest rank, making them worthy of supreme bliss."[14] While being a parish priest, living outside a monastery, and being constantly among people in the world, Father Ilarion succeeded in preserving himself spotless from the world[15] and, at the conclusion of his earthly life, in ascending to that height inscrutable for us, to which he had begun ascending in the years of his youth.

According to the commandment of Christ the Savior, Christians are called to be "the salt of the earth" and "the light of the world,"[16] that men "may see [their] good works, and glorify [their] Father in heaven."[17] Father Ilarion was such a Christian, illumined with an otherworldly light. He was that lighted lamp that is not put "under a basket, but on a lampstand, and it gives light to all who are in the house."[18] In the gloom of ecclesiastical collapse, in the days of human tribulations, he shone upon all, preserving souls from despondency, despair, and disillusionment. He taught that outside the Lord, the heart has no true peace anywhere on earth, and he himself sought strengthening of his infirmities in God alone. For us, he was a guiding star, which strove to rise ever higher. He knew no limits: The more greatly a person was endowed, the stricter, more exacting, and more unbending Father Ilarion would be. Yet, his mercy also knew no bounds. In an instant, by a gentle, affectionate glance or word, he would loose the overburdened soul's load, as it were, and off that soul would soar across the sky, free as a bird.

As R.B.N. recalled,

> Naturally, among us, the members of Father's spiritual family, there were also incidents of divisive rivalry and discontent. He knew our infirmities, and with all his might he strove to overcome divisions, revealing to each what and as much as that person was capable of hearing, understanding, and taking to heart with faith, lovingly perceiving our needs and sending us every kind of help. He loved God; hence, he also loved his flock, and suffered greatly from the lack of love caused by the jealousies and envies that overcame inexperienced souls. He always had a single answer to the "discord of this world": love one another (John 15:17).

Father Ilarion frequently called to mind the apostle's words, that he who has not love is as "sounding brass or a clanging cymbal,"[19] but "he who abides in love abides in God, and God in him."[20] If people had love, the whole Christian world would be one, after the manner of the unity of the Radiant Trinity.[21]

However, as Father emphasized, love is unattainable without humility; hence, following the ascetics, he strove to go the way of humble mindedness. Year after year in his sermons, he would tell of the great ascetic Anthony the Great, who labored in the fourth century in Egypt, to whom a model of spiritual perfection was revealed. Once, during prayer, he heard the voice of God: "Anthony, you have not yet attained the stature of a certain tanner living in Alexandria." Anthony hastened to Alexandria, and finding the tanner, asked him to tell him of his good works. The latter, however, knew nothing good of himself, and for this reason, both when rising from his bed early in the morning and when lying down to sleep at night, he would repeat, "All the dwellers of this city, from the greatest to the least, shall enter the Kingdom of Heaven for their virtues. I alone will go into eternal torment for my sins." Upon hearing the tanner's words, the blessed Anthony replied, "Truly, my son, you, like a skilled jeweler, sitting quietly in your home, have attained the Kingdom of God. While I, though I have spent my whole life in the desert, have not attained spiritual reason and have not achieved the stature of consciousness that your words express."

Beside all else, Father Ilarion had a great fear of God, which in any strained situation was reborn in him into God's love. Exhausted with weeping for himself and his sins, he would fall down in tears before the all-perfect Father, "who is Love," and be filled with horror, realizing his own unworthiness before Him, and this fear would then be transfigured into the fullness of love. Father used approximately these words in one of his sermons to explain the essence of the fear of God, which he understood to be the beginning not only of wisdom but also of love.

All of the above are the fruits of Father Ilarion's profound love for people, and his mercy and compassion for them. As one French philosopher wrote, telling a person, "I love you," is the same as saying, "You will live forever; you will never die"; for according to the Apostle Paul, "love never fails."[22] This is the kind of love we felt toward ourselves; that is, through the power of Father's love for us, we felt our own immortality. Having once experienced this love for ourselves, we could no longer sink into oblivion or die for eternity. It would be ridiculous and absurd! It is not for nothing that even after our dear Father's repose, we continue to experience an intensely burning connection with him.

Father Ilarion's monastic and priestly path was founded on the principles that lead to renunciation of everything that could hinder love for God and neighbor. He constantly repeated what the Lord spoke of at the Last Supper to his disciples, of which the apostles said, "And above all things have fervent love for one another, for 'love will cover a multitude of sins.'.... As every one has received a gift, minister it to one another, as good stewards of the manifold grace of God."[23]

Feeling Father's love for them and seeing that he had access to another world, people hurried to entrust their souls to him. The Glinsk elders taught us to "be a burning candle!."[24] Father was that burning candle, whose flame consumed the sins of penitents. Lit by his candle, they experienced hitherto unknown feelings of moral renewal and faith in God.

Father placed a high value on purity of body and soul, which is so very rare. For this reason, he particularly revered his young novice Irina for her inward and outward piety, uprightness, chastity, and industriousness, as well as her sensitivity to the moral condition of the Sunday school children, and her constant search for the best means of their spiritual and moral upbringing. By the same token, as Father's favorite child, she was scolded more than the others on account of other self-affirming young novices, and even had to endure slander.

CHAPTER 15

A Confessor of Souls

CONFESSION

Confessions with Father Ilarion were unforgettable. In order to be heard, one had to carefully prepare what one needed to confess ahead of time. Father did not permit the penitent to bury the facts in verbosity. If the latter continued talking, he would interrupt and turn attention to the penitent's inner life.

Due to his God-given clairvoyance, he would frequently name the penitent's sins himself, considerably supplementing those named by the latter, but he constantly reminded the sinner of the benefits of self-reproof, which would cleanse one's soul and reestablish one's connection with God. He would explain that one must confess so as to cultivate a disgust for sin in the soul, so that sin would become hateful. Occasionally, he would cite examples from his own life, responding to questions which, although unasked, worried his parishioners. He accused himself as the chief among sinners, thereby giving that person pause and forcing him or her to look within more deeply and strictly.

Irina Vladimirovna Smirnova recalled confession with Father:

> Before listing the sins at general confession he would always give a short exhortation, during which the heart would soften and be humbled. Frequently, tears would well up in your eyes, and you felt an immense desire to recount your sins sincerely, without any self-justification. Father frequently urged us not to soothe ourselves and rest on our laurels, as is our sinful nature. In struggling with this extremely widespread spiritual infirmity throughout his

life, Father was strict and demanding primarily with himself, and only then with those who wished to imitate him in spiritual self-improvement. After scolding somebody roundly he would pray for that person for a long time, and the latter would either return to struggle with his sins and passions, or leave for good (though Father nevertheless continued to pray for him, and the person would usually return).

Father Ilarion carefully guarded people from any justification of their sins whatsoever. In one of his sermons, he recounted a story that occurred with a certain monk on the first day of Great Lent:

He happened to find an egg, and his peaceful spiritual disposition was upset. It seemed a pity to throw it away; after all, it was someone's offering. To give it to someone would be to lead that person into sin. So he decided to eat it himself, so as not to waste good food. Since no fires were lit in the kitchen during the first week, he had the idea of cooking the egg over a candle flame. At that moment the abbot came to visit him. Finding the monk thus strangely occupied, the clairvoyant elder asked him:

"Dear brother, exactly what are you doing, and why are you doing this? Have you forgotten that it is now Lent, and that the fare you are preparing is not eaten during this time? Do you not agree? For you know that Lent has been appointed since apostolic times, according to Christ's words: 'He shall be taken from them, and then they shall fast!'"

"Yes, Father, I know that it is now Lent, and that eating this is forbidden, but the devil tempted me, teaching me this craft."

Suddenly, however, the devil, who had been sitting right there behind the stove, indignantly retorted:

"That sin's a new one to me! Here I've been sitting behind the stove, studying how you can cook an egg over a candle!"

From such stories, the penitents were expected to draw useful lessons.

Whatever life's circumstances, Father called people not to despond or despair, but to pray, have fear of God, repent, and hope on the will of God. He always reminded people that there is no sin that could surpass God's mercy, except for blasphemy against the

Holy Spirit. He frequently cited the Gospel parable about the lost sheep, which its master went to seek, leaving the other ninety-nine sheep in the hills, and the Savior's words about the joy in heaven over a single repentant sinner, which is greater than over ninety-nine righteous men.[1] He invited people to make a firm resolution for a new life through repentance. "Say, 'I won't do that anymore—I won't!'" he would frequently say to the penitent, moving him or her to a sincere desire to repent and remain faithful to the promise.

Penances were served for the penitents' correction. Many rightly perceived these penances not as punishments but as God's orders—His treatment for the correction of the internal distortion caused by sin. Through Father Ilarion, the Lord Himself would invite a person to repair and restore his relationship with Him. Father Ilarion adapted the penances he imposed to the state of the penitent's heart and the depths of one's sorrow, maintaining a level which one's heart and mind could receive, so as not to harm oneself or dampen one's good inclinations. Many of us deserved penances far greater than we could have borne, and Father bore them for us himself by making prostrations without number, lighting candles, praying, and crucifying himself for others. It is no accident that the doctors who examined the X-rays of his heart were bewildered by how many hours he lived on earth.

Yet, what confessions Father held during Great Lent! As Galina Petrovna Lashutina recalled,

> Every Clean Saturday of the first week of Great Lent, Father Ilarion held confession. This was an unforgettable event, and I recall it now with warm tears. Nothing and no one can replace it. On the solea stand sixty people, sometime more—nearly all Father Ilarion's spiritual children. I read the prayers of repentance, stumbling from my abundant tears, and Fr Ilarion, standing amid his children, pronounces the sins of each who comes under his epitrachelion. All are weeping, tears streaming down their faces, and many are sobbing, which those who confess to a different priest find greatly moving.
>
> All this imprinted itself in my heart's memory for the rest of my life.

To those around him, Father frequently seemed incomprehensible and obscure. People's consciousness could not comprehend the spiritual measure allotted him by God. Sometimes he would refuse to confess a person who had otherwise prepared but made a seemingly insignificant blunder. Yet, at other times, he would receive a person to confession who had not prepared whatsoever.

Father Ilarion gave particular attention to young people and to those who were in church for the first time, whatever their age. When a person had come to confession and was about to commune without having prepared in the least for these great sacraments, he was quite vocal in his indignation: "My, my, you certainly live well! No fasting, no praying, no labor whatsoever—and here you come to call at God's temple! Go on, get on out of here.... There's nothing to discuss.... I have millions like you!" (This last always made the regular parishioners smile.) If the neophyte penitents took even a step back, however, they would hear, "Where do you think you're going ... ?! Stand over there," pushing them into a corner behind him, "and pray ... !"

These catechumens would get their turns after everyone else had confessed, and with what skill, care, and love Father confessed them! After growling and scolding them to maintain the fear of God, he would first cleanse and scrub their souls from top to bottom so that, steamed and cleansed from this "sauna," people would return to their homes profoundly grateful and with tears in their eyes. They would remember that day for the rest of their lives. For many, the first meeting with Father Ilarion proved decisive and fateful, and the church became their home. People began to believe in the future life with all their heart and to love it.

To ensure that his longstanding and newly acquired spiritual children were not growing cold in the work of pleasing God, "that each one ... show the same diligence to the full assurance of hope until the end, that [they] do not become sluggish,"[2] Father Ilarion would periodically call them on the phone, inquiring, "Do you pray? Do you cry any tears? Were you at the morning or evening service at any church? Did you read your morning and evening prayers? What did you do that day?" What answer could we careless ones make without falling into yet another sin? Yet, the soul would acknowledge and be distressed by its guilt and its poverty, and would be spurred to contrite repentance and good works.

One spiritual daughter remembered acutely how, during her first year after coming to Father, she had to write down all her sins in detail. Father Ilarion took the whole notebook home with him. A week passed in painful anticipation of his reaction to what may be called a life's confession. It seemed that now he would never accept such a revolting, sinful person. Father, however, absolved the load of sins burdening her soul with such love, understanding, and compassion that her heart was filled once and for all with warm, profound gratitude for God's limitless mercy, as manifested through Father. Many years later, he would joke, "Remember how you used to bring me those full-length books of yours?" Only later came the realization that, as Holy Scripture states, "Those who are well have no need of a physician, but those who are sick."[3]

Being a true monk, Father Ilarion did not apply the severe forms of monastic life to his spiritual children. He understood that one can be saved or perish both in monasticism and in the world, and that the most important thing is to love those whom the Lord has put near you. This seemingly simplest of arts in actuality proved the most difficult for his flock.

Here we refer to the notes of one of Father's spiritual daughters, Anna Mikhailovna Gorlova:

> Today, on March 7, 2009, I came home from the service feeling deeply dissatisfied: had I confessed, or had I not? The young priest took my list of sins, and said: "You've repented of all these things; why list them to me?" I, however, had a great need to confess aloud before the Lord. He repeated what he had said, and concluded by saying, "Goodbye." Naturally, tears welled up in my eyes. I recalled how Father had confessed, and the profound sense of responsibility with which he treated everything, especially confession....
>
> Another occurrence comes to mind. Once I was confessing in one of the Novgorod monasteries. I had listed my sins on three pages, and had prepared for a wholehearted confession. The

priest, however, didn't even glance at my list, and wouldn't listen to me. I returned home very upset, and called Father Ilarion. Upon hearing my story, he replied: "Yes, that priest took a good deal upon himself."

Father himself confessed very thoroughly. Once, during the first years of his time in Bronnitsa, I was sick and had a high temperature. I came to him for confession, but my thoughts were a jumble, and I couldn't get the words out. Father said, "Let's pray together." He knelt down, and I knelt beside him. And such penitential weeping came over me.... Never in my life have I communed like that. It was so easy, so good. It was unforgettable.

Each year in the church, the rite of the sacrament of unction was served. This rite dates back to apostolic times: "Is anyone among you sick? Let him call for the elders of the church, and let them pray over him, anointing him with oil in the name of the Lord. And the prayer of faith will save the sick, and the Lord will raise him up. And if he has committed sins, he will be forgiven."[4] In sending the apostles to preach, the Lord "gave them power over unclean spirits.... So they went out and preached that people should repent. And they cast out many demons, and anointed with oil many who were sick, and healed them."[5]

Frequently, the common people were afraid of unction, believing that it led to death. This attitude appeared under the Soviet government, when everything related to ecclesiastical rituals was considered agitation. People received unction only at the end of their lives, and then in secret, and usually only solitary elderly people, who did not need to worry about their relatives' social standing. This is why each time, in the usual sermon on the eve of the rite of unction, Father Ilarion would give a detailed explanation in plain language of the meaning of this ecclesiastical ritual. In this way, each person participating experienced his inclusion, through the grace of the Holy Spirit bestowed in the sacrament, in "righteousness and peace and joy in the Holy Spirit,"[6] and the meaning and significance of sicknesses, sufferings, and death—God's providence—were revealed to each in his or her own measure.

We cannot pass over Father Ilarion's position as confessor of the Novgorod Diocese, to which he was appointed in 1981. In his 1987 report on confession of the clergy, His Eminence Metropolitan Alexey placed the following resolution:[7] "I thank Fr Archimandrite for his labor in confessing the clergy of the Novgorod Diocese."

In November 2008, Archpriest Mikhail Lozhkov, Dean of Khvoinaya Okrug and Rector of St Nicholas Church, shared his recollections of confession with Father Ilarion at the Novgorod Diocese:

"Our meetings with Father Ilarion were very interesting, especially when I would come to him in Novgorod to confess (from 1993 to last year). The meeting would take place well before confession began. Father gave very valuable spiritual counsels, which I tried to implement in my spiritual practice. For example, a certain issue arose with regard to my children. Prayer and composure, Father said. And indeed, the question was soon resolved—everything fell into place.

"I once said to Father Ilarion that I was thinking of monasticism, and asked his blessing for my wife and myself to live together as brother and sister. I now live according to the monastic rule. With Father's blessing I went to the bishop to ask to be tonsured, but the bishop did not give his blessing. 'Well, then,' said Father Ilarion, 'it isn't yet time for you to become a monk.'

"One time, in 2007, when as usual I arrived very early for confession, Father Ilarion gave me his jeweled pectoral cross, which was clearly handmade, and blessed me with it: 'Here, take it, and continue carrying your cross.'

"The most important thing in his talks was instruction on complete prayer, on not abbreviating the services under any pretense, on serving as often as possible, and, no matter how hard it might be, continuing to pray. I constantly recall this with gratitude, and strive to implement his instructions in my life.

"At our meetings he constantly asked about our health and recommended that we tend it with care—much service to God and men still lay ahead.

"His instructions for the work of our pastoral life were and still are very meaningful. What a pity it is that such bright beacons as Father Ilarion leave this life. Even a single word from him could help resolve a complicated spiritual issue for an entire year.

"With profound gratitude and love I recall our brief meetings and conversations, and every word Father bestowed upon this young priest. The moment you came to confession he would immediately say: 'Oh, Father Mikhail's here! You're the one that's snagged four churches—or is it five now?' And no matter what he said, his every word breathed love, compassion, and sympathy. Priests of various ages would come to confession, but he confessed everyone in their turn, while observing etiquette, showing respect for both age and gray hair. No one took offense; everyone was content. I think that every priest, not just myself, went away from confession winged and inspired: one wanted again and again to serve God and men, to work, and to pray.

"Today, although half a year has passed since Father Ilarion left this earthly life, when you turn to him for help, you acutely sense him there beside you. You feel his warmth, his grace-imbued help, and with all your heart you understand: in departing unto life eternal Father did not leave us. Each time when I begin praying for the health and repose of the servants of God at the service, I catch my hands and my heart refusing to remove a particle for his repose, wanting to remove one for his health. You have the sense that Father is in a hospital somewhere and will soon return—that on the feast of Pascha or of Christ's Nativity he will come to the church, and once again you'll see his irrepressible figure among the other priests, and once again you'll hear that voice so dear to your heart, his good advice, and his entreaty: 'Pray, pray, fulfill your prayer rule, pray for your neighbor!'

"I thank the Lord for the joy of having met so spiritual a person on my life's path as Father Ilarion, whom I consider my most important spiritual father on earth."

Below are several excerpts from an interview[8] that Father gave to T. Kulpinova, special correspondent for the Novgorod Diocese, which touch on both Father's spiritual fatherhood and his views on today's generation of young people who have come to the Church:

Kulpinova: Your Reverence, all the priests of the diocese confess to you. No doubt they don't just confess, but also turn to you for advice. What advice do you give most often?

Father: I'd like to cite the example of Anthony the Great, and how he taught one person to pity people and be lenient with them. "Put an arrow in your bow and pull it back," he told him. The latter did so. Anthony said he wasn't pulling it back far enough, and kept on saying so until the hunter said, "No further, or it will break." Anthony replied, "So it is in God's work. If you overburden your brethren's strength, they will soon fall away from God's work. From time to time you must be lenient with them."

Kulpinova: So you hold that a merciful priest is preferable to a severe one?

Father: Preferable? Yes, you could say that. The times dictate this preference—troubled, uncertain, not guaranteeing so much as a crust of bread. Add to this seventy years of godlessness, with an adult population that not only doesn't know "Our Father" by heart, but can't even pronounce "Lord, have mercy." How far will you get without mercy? The only way is by instructing, by comforting and pitying. Sometimes a person has absolutely no one to pity him except the Church. He comes here for warmth, for light, and he mustn't be pushed away, but rather shown warmth and affection.

Kulpinova: So, who comes to the Church today? Has its contingent changed?

Father: It has. Now the majority of people that come are not old ladies, but rather people of the middle generation, who have already seen something of life and come to a realization. Many of them are educated and well-off. The fact is, when a person finds no place for himself—the most widespread diagnosis today—when he is tossed about in search of himself, no material thing can fill the void in his soul. This void, this vacuum that has formed between a person's life and his soul can only be filled by the Lord, only by conversing with Him, and by prayer—whether private or by the book doesn't matter, as long as it is sincere, ardent, tearful. When the heart opens up in this kind of prayer, a person feels joy, and sweetness, and silence, and peace—all the good things in the world.

Kulpinova: Father Ilarion, your ministry spans over ten generations. How would you label the current generation?

Father: I would label it a generation of spiritual laxity and drowsiness, of coarseness of heart.

Kulpinova: Is there an antidote?

Father: There is. Ignatius Brianchaninov wrote much about it, as did John of Kronstadt. Humility, sincere repentance, and washing with tears conquer all. A believer who has sinned doesn't start asking whether he can atone for his sin by prayer—he simply starts praying without thinking. To pray is to rise above sin. Archpriest Alexey Mechev of Moscow once said: "Do not be afraid when you fall. Be afraid when you do not get up."

Kulpinova: Your Reverence, young priests serve with you in this church, and many young people come to confess to you. The priestly brethren have grown younger in recent years. Is this a good thing in your opinion, or not?

Father: I, for one, planned to spend my whole life in a monastery. Whether it's a good or a bad thing that it didn't turn out that way, I don't know. But I've put my whole soul into this parish, and I'll leave here feet first. Thirty years ago churches, schools, and seminaries were being closed, and there weren't enough priests.

Is it a good thing or not? It is, and it isn't. Sometimes a young priest is better educated, more zealous, and more soulful than one who is old and experienced. Experience, of course, counts for a lot, but it's hardly everything. But soul—no experience, or extensive knowledge, or even extensive wisdom can take its place. Metropolitan Nikodim once said: "Pastorship without soul is a waterless spring that cannot quench one's thirst."

Father's monastic path was based on the principles that lead to the great mystery of God's love, and to renunciation of everything that could hinder him from loving God and neighbor. He constantly repeated what the Lord spoke of to His disciples at the Last Supper, of which the apostle spoke, "And above all things have fervent love for one another, for 'love will cover a multitude of sins.'... As every one has received a gift, minister it to one another, as good stewards of the manifold grace of God."[9]

It was typical of Father to end a sermon on the day of his patron saint (October 21/November 3) with these words: "In conclusion, I wish to cite the text of one ancient prayer:

O Lord my God, vouchsafe me to be an instrument of Thy peace,

That may I bring love to where there is hatred,

That may I forgive where people offend,

That may I unite where there is contention,

That may I speak the truth where error reigns,

That I may raise up faith where doubt crushes,

That I may rouse hope where despair torments,

That I may bring light into darkness,

That I may raise up joy where sorrow dwells.

O Lord my God, vouchsafe not that I be comforted, but that I may comfort,

Not that I be understood, but that I may understand others,

Not that I be loved, but that I may love others.

For whoever gives, receives,

Whoever forgets himself, acquires,

Whoever forgives will be forgiven,

And whoever dies awakens in life eternal.

Amen![10]

CHAPTER 16

The Patriarch and the Pilgrims

A VISIT FROM THE PATRIARCH

On May 3, 1990, His Holiness Patriarch Pimen went to the Lord, and His Holiness Alexey II was elected to the patriarchal throne. Soon after his enthronement, the newly elected Primate of the Russian Church came to Novgorod. On August 16, 1991, in the ancient Novgorodian Sophia, after long years of forced inactivity, the Divine Liturgy was served for the first time. A rainbow shining directly over the cathedral at that moment appeared as a benevolent sign of the rebirth of spiritual life. A beautiful poster depicting it was soon printed. Upon seeing it, Father asked, "How come I don't have that rainbow?" It was promptly presented to him, and it hung thereafter in his cell.

During his visit to the Novgorodian land, the primate also visited the Bronnitsa Transfiguration of the Lord Church. For Father Ilarion, his vast flock, and all the inhabitants of the nearby towns and villages, this was a great occasion. How many joyous preparations there were and how much excitement! How Father rejoiced at the honor that had become his, to receive in his church His Holiness, who was so ardently loved and deeply revered! The reverberations of this momentous occasion excited Father's soul to the end of his days. Still, they enliven the hearts of all the church's parishoners and the inhabitants of all the region of Novgorod.

In answer to the question of a correspondent for the diocesan newspaper *Sophia* regarding his evaluation of contemporary parish life, its current state, and its future, the Patriarch responded,

"Full-blooded parish life is the foundation of the spiritual well-being of the Church as a whole. How successfully that life develops, be it of even the smallest community, determines both the present and the future of our Church."[1] Apparently, it was primarily this full-blooded parish life at the Bronnitsa Transfiguration of the Lord Church for which His Holiness revered Father Ilarion and regarded him with great affection. When Father reposed, His Holiness was saddened that he had not been notified immediately.

PILGRIMAGES

Father loved to make pilgrimages, particularly in the summer for vacation. As Mother Valentina recalled, "Father visited many holy places. He traveled to Georgia to see elders Andronik and Seraphim while they were still alive, and later to visit their graves. He was at the alleged place of the crucifixion of Holy Apostle Simon of Canaan,[2] and at the place where Saint John Chrysostom is buried,[3] and went to venerate the relics of Holy Equal-to-the-Apostles Nina, enlightener of Georgia[4] and Venerable David Garejeli.[5]

"Father visited other holy places, as well: Zagorsk (Sergiev Posad), Diveevo, the Optina Hermitage, Pechora, Pyukhtitsa, Voronezh, Pochaev, and many other places."

In 1995, Father Ilarion traveled to Moscow to venerate a copy of the Iveron Icon of the Mother of God from the Iveron Monastery on Athos. Father greatly revered this icon, a reverence he inherited from the Glinsk Hermitage, and it was located on the first, local-veneration tier of the iconostas in the Bronnitsa church.

On April 26, 1996, with great ceremony, Russia greeted the relics of Holy Great-Martyr and Healer Panteleimon from Holy Mount Athos. Father Ilarion immediately hastened to Moscow to pay homage to this saint, who has been revered since ancient times, and to venerate his healing relics in the Theophany Cathedral. In this way, as it were, he was united with Holy Mount Athos, for which his ardent soul had always longed. In 2000, the honorable head of the Healer Panteleimon was brought to Russia a second time, and Father Ilarion, now gravely ill, was able once again to offer ardent prayers that his infirmities be eased and to venerate the holy relics of the great martyr, this time in St Petersburg. Along with him, we all prayed fervently to the all-merciful physician for Father's health.

In 2004, he traveled to venerate an icon greatly revered in Russia: the Tikhvin Icon of the Mother of God,[6] returned from the United States to the holy monastery in Tikhvin, which was being restored.

CHAPTER 17

Charisma

Many testified to the charismatic personality and clairvoyance of Father Ilarion. As Vladyka Luka, superior of the Glinsk Hermitage, recalled,

> One of the gifts with which the Lord rewarded Father ... was the gift of clairvoyance. In testimony of this I will relate something that happened to me. It was on the eve of the feast of Pascha. When I received congratulations on the feast, all addressed me as a bishop: "Dear Most Reverend...." Only Father Ilarion wrote: "Dear Very Most Reverend...," addressing me as an archbishop. I thought that he or his secretary had made a mistake. But it was I who was mistaken, for on the second day of Pascha I was summoned to Kiev, where at the evening service, at the entrance, His Eminence Metropolitan Vladimir elevated me to the rank of archbishop.
>
> Father's words regarding our monastery are also coming to pass, though we thought it impossible, and that he was merely comforting us: the monastery is being revived.

Many suspected Father Ilarion's gift of clairvoyance and became convinced of it by their own experiences. However, in his deep humility, he never displayed it openly, as though it did not exist at all, as noted by Nun Eufemia: "Father concealed his clairvoyance, playing the fool. One time he was sitting with his spiritual children, who were evaluating each other's work. I was sitting on the floor, wondering why Father was joking around, and thinking he would do better to tell us something interesting, or read to us, or sing. He got up, and as he walked by he rapped on my head: 'Oh, but I have been telling them something interesting, and singing, and reading—about you!' He added: 'Elena's skirt is knee-length skirt, but ought to be ankle-length.' Soon after that I began wearing ankle-length skirts."

Schemanun Mikhaila recalled that Father played a key role in her life: "One priest, knowing that I wanted to enter a monastery, invited me to go with him instead. Father Ilarion, however, said that if I went with him I would remain in the world: 'Go to a monastery. There you'll be a true nun,' he said. I was tonsured in Pyukhtina Monastery, and I recall Fr Ilarion with gratitude."

Galina Petrovna Lashutina recalled Father's influence on those around her

Many things about him amazed me, but particularly his wise and intelligent approach to every parishioner. First he would greet the person amiably and affectionately, and ask about various aspects of his life. Father would then begin to see him with his spiritual mind and vision. I was always amazed and wondered at his mental intellect and insight. You just had to hear and understand it. And when he blessed you, and spoke just a word or two, you experienced an extraordinary state of renewal. His words were strengthened by the grace that proceeded from him.

There where instances when, during the Divine Liturgy, the other parishioners and I saw Father illumined with a fiery radiance, and at those moments one believed that angels were serving with him. It was impossible to look with bodily eyes. In some measure his condition passed on to all the worshipers in the church. It felt as though you were standing on air.

I wish to testify to this with certainty: the Holy Spirit and the grace of God constantly abode over his house, over the church, and over the entire church territory. This was felt not only by the regular parishioners, but even by those who came from various cities. People frequently asked why it was so easy to breathe in and around the church, why the mind and heart were concentrated in prayer, and you felt yourself as though born again. The answer was that Father Ilarion breathed God's grace upon every worshiper. It was by his blessing and prayer that a handful of people could perform more work (not only without tiring, but even with a sense of a special influx of strength and inspiration) than two or three dozen people could have managed. He knew everything, saw everything, sensed everything. How could it really have been otherwise, when he burned constantly like a burning bush?

Vera Aleksandrovna Moskvina recalled Father's effect on her family:

In 1978, at Father's invitation, my 14-year-old son Evgeny and I went to see Father Ilarion.

The moment we entered his house, he turned to my son and asked: "Zhenka, you smoke?!" My son tried to deny it, but you couldn't fool Father. I had never suspected this, and if anyone else had said so I would not have believed it. We spent three days with Father, then prepared to return home. I was living in Severodvinsk at the time, and the next day I was supposed to return to work. The journey was not an easy one: we had to take a bus, then a train, and then a plane, and in winter, at that. Father blessed us for our journey. From Novgorod to Leningrad, however, no public transportation was running due to heavy snows. We wandered back and forth between bus and train stations, as the hours went by. Then a man approached me and asked whether I needed to go to Leningrad. He seated us in his car, and we rode with him the rest of the way.

Father always prayed for anyone leaving on a journey. Anna (Zhuravleva) was there at the time. She later wrote that while we were standing at the station Father was praying at home. Suddenly, he said: "You know, Galinka is mad at me and scolding. She'll calm down soon, though; everything will be alright." Later, when we were already on the airplane, he said again: "Now they'll be home quite soon." I compared the times of the events: it was our dear Father's prayers that cleared the way for us, and at precisely the time of which Anna wrote.

Vladimir Veselyev also remembered how Father Ilarion's charisma affected his family:

During perestroika, many businesses began to collapse. I was working at a meat processing plant, and layoffs began. Production began to drop. I asked Father whether I might go to a different job. He blessed me, but then, after a moment's thought, added: "The meat processing plant won't collapse, though." And indeed, in time it began flourishing.

One time my mother was sitting, holding Father's photograph in her hands and talking with him. Seeing a hole in her dress, she said aloud: "Father, you might send me some cloth to make a dress." Time went by, and she forgot the matter. Then one day some people came from Father to see Mother Eufemia, and told her: "Here; Father sent this to you, and said for you to take it to Paraskeva; it's something she asked for." When my mother saw the very cloth she had wanted, she wept with joy, and recalled her request before Father's photograph. This shows how much God gave Father to see. . . .

Once, at a moleben, Father called me over and asked: "Vladimir, is your brother ill?" "Yes." How he prayed then! He prayed so that my brother's intense headaches ceased, and he stopped blacking out.

Handmaid of God Elena S. recounted a similar instance of Father's clairvoyance:

Around 1989–1991 I unexpectedly got a letter from Father in which he inquired: "Write immediately and tell me what has happened now, you martyr." His question hit me like a thunderbolt. I had not complained of my sorrows to him before, and suddenly he himself was asking. As it happened, I had indeed again met with a great sorrow. My first feeling was of profound gratitude, followed closely by profound amazement. I wrote what had happened to me, and asked him not to write to me like that any more, since no one pitied me and my heart might not withstand such sympathy for my grief. Father didn't ask anymore, and I didn't complain. And if anything happened to me, I would write to him briefly about it (he asked only that I mention the person's name).

The handmaid of God Klavdia (Bronnitsa) attested to Father Ilarion's gift of sight:

I want so very much to write about what I have begun to suspect. Archimandrite Ilarion is not just a priest: he is a seer. Here is what happened: the enemy of the human race does not sleep, constantly seeking a way into our souls. Two prosphora bakers, Klavdia (myself) and Valentina, quarreled, so badly that Father had to intervene. When he saw us, he cried: "I saw the devil above you, and he was prevailing. I wondered: what will happen? Will my prosphora bakers withstand, or not?" We did not withstand. Father Ilarion covered us with his epitrachelion. We fell to our knees, asking his and each other's forgiveness. Father gave us his hands, and raised us up one after the other. We went off to the bakery to bake prosphora.

As noted by Elena Chistyakova, "I recall how before one moleben Father Ilarion approached me and asked: 'Elena, is everything alright at home?' 'Yes, Father, thank God, by your prayers,' I replied. A few minutes later Father again asked me the same question. That evening, while fixing the car, my husband was nearly killed through carelessness. It was a miracle for my husband Evgeny and for myself that he lived. I was certain that Father Ilarion had been praying for us, and by his prayers had prevented a tragedy for our family."

Nadezhda Wegh was also awed by Father's foresight:

Father's clairvoyance amazed me. Once I became seriously ill, to the point that I began fainting, and I was having considerable trouble with both my son and my father. It was Lent at the time. I felt terrible emotionally, physically, and spiritually. Lying on my bed, I thought: "I think I'll have a bit of kielbasa; perhaps that will help." Somehow or other I got up from my bed, made my way to the refrigerator, and began eating the kielbasa. Before I had even finished, the phone rang. It was Father. "Listen here, Nadezhda, you can be on your deathbed, but don't you eat meat during Great Lent!" Well, I thought, it's just like in the fairy tale: "Don't sit on the stump, don't eat any cakes."[1] Father sees and knows everything....

Once it was my birthday. I had come to the monastery to commune, and felt so poorly that all I could do in church was sit—I hadn't the strength to stand. I approached the icon of the Mother of God, and asked her: "Mother of God, I'm feeling so bad right now... perhaps I've not long left to live. Won't you reveal to me how long

I have left? Perhaps then I'll take better care of my soul." I communed and returned home. No sooner had I removed my coat when Father Ilarion called and congratulated me on my birthday, singing "Many Years." "You'll live to be forty-seven," he said, and again sang "Many Years." At first I was delighted at hearing my spiritual father's response to the question I had asked the Most-Holy Mother of God. Then, however, I fell into temptation and began to grumble, thinking: "Well, that's a fine thing—the rest of my family sin with all their five senses, pursue their careers, and earn awards, and in two years I'll be dead and with no award but a gold coffin." I began grumbling about my husband, and my son, and Father Ilarion. Then, once again, I heard words of comfort over the phone: "I am praying for many, many years for you." Gradually I began to recover, and was almost completely restored to health. Glory to God for all things....

Once I was having a very difficult time. I did not know how to go on living. I mentally went over all my acquaintances: who was I to rely on, and whose example ought I to follow in life? "I'll live as I know how, as best I can," I decided. "I'll follow no one's example, and ask no one for help. They're all barely alive themselves—old, sick, and infirm." No sooner had I thought this when Father Ilarion called. "Follow my example—mine, Alexandra's, Valentina's. Rely on us, ask us for help; pray to the Holy Fathers to make you wiser." Many, many times Father amazed and comforted us by his responsiveness and clairvoyance. May his memory be eternal.

CHAPTER 18

In the Holy Land:
The Garden of Gethsemane

A special page in the spiritual chronicle of Father Ilarion's life is his blessed pilgrimage to the Holy Land during Holy Week of 1999. This good intention and ardent desire came upon him, by his own admission, long ago in 1941, when in the city of Starodub, Orlov Region (present-day Bryansk Region), he met Nun Amvrosia, who told him of her year-long sojourn in the Holy Land, and of the descent of the Holy Fire upon the Lord's tomb.

Nearly six decades later, Father recalled,

> With great excitement and awe I listened to her tale, which resurrected in my heart a passionate desire to visit the Holy Land, to approach the holy places, to kiss them, to water them with my tears and give thanks, and to pray. However, the spirit of the times, various external circumstances, and ceaseless ecclesiastical duties did not appear to favor the fulfillment of this ardently desired intent.
>
> But then the winds of change blew up, and nearly six decades since that time they swept me like a blade of grass from my bed of sickness and, thank the Lord, carried me as though on a fairy-tale carpet to the Promised Land. My dearest dream, hidden in the recesses of my heart, yet which nothing had ever destroyed, had come true.[1]

Father gave fervent thanks to the Lord for His mercy in being vouchsafed to visit the promised land and, "setting foot upon it himself, had ... the bold idea of describing what he saw ... in the hope that it might be of some small benefit to the Christian soul."[2] In 2001, he wrote *In the Promised Land: An Edifying Account of a Pilgrimage to the Holy City of Jerusalem and Other Holy Places*. He willingly gave it away, hoping thereby to animate people's hearts. Indeed, it aroused many to newness of life.

The book begins brightly and with great inspiration:

> Truly there is no other land on earth which could unite with such grace all that is especially dear to the Christian heart, which could embody the living Book of Genesis, and, most importantly, which reveals the Savior to the world. Here, in the eternally new Holy City of Jerusalem, permeated with the rays of the glory of Christ's Resurrection, the holy things which every believing person holds most precious are to be found....
>
> Twenty centuries have gone by since the time when our Lord Jesus Christ lived on earth. Many events have taken place here over the years. Much has been built and rebuilt, and much cannot be replaced or restored....
>
> Nonetheless, this is the very same Holy Land of our Savior, wholly trodden by His most-pure feet, and saturated with His sacrificial blood—the Land which the most-pure little feet of the Most-Holy Mother of God touched, and which still remembers the Prophets, Apostles, and Evangelists. This land is linked with the entire history of the salvation of the human race, and each clump of earth, every stone here, bears witness to this....
>
> On this land, "over the barriers,"[3] heedless of time and space, the centuries float from afar to meet you and stand before one so clearly and visibly that you feel yourself not only a viewer and witness, but a direct participant in them in the omnipresence of Christ Himself: for always and everywhere He is here beside you. Hence, in our time of nationwide trials, when it seems that the people have reached the end of their strength, from all sides they come streaming to the Sacred Palestinian Land, to find strength in the unflagging grace and mercy of the Lord.[4]

The most inspired pages of the book are dedicated to the wonder of the descent of the Holy Fire in the Lord's tomb on Holy Saturday morning: "The Lord vouchsafed me also to taste of the unearthly joy of comfort at the Holy Tomb. On Holy Saturday evening I found myself in the Cubiculum, where I joined the Greek monks in changing the vesture on the Lord's Tomb. The drops of grace-imbued dew, left after the descent of the Holy Fire, had not yet dried, and I smelt an unusual fragrance, and such joy, such peace and calm penetrated my soul that I forgot everything."⁵

Upon returning home to Bronnitsa, he reverently recalled his sojourn in the Holy Land:

The Holy Land now lies behind me, and before me the sea surges and crashes, like our life upon the earth.... Again and again we give fervent thanks to the Lord our God and His Most-pure Mother, who have vouchsafed us to visit this blessed land, and realize with sadness that it is impossible to see all the holy places in such a short time. Hence, at 4:30 in the afternoon we rise into the air with the cherished holy treasures of the Promised Land locked away deep in our hearts, and in the fervent hope of returning here once again.

Farewell, my beloved, my desired Jerusalem, most holy city .... The Gornensky mothers saw the departing pilgrims off with a song of farewell: "Let my right hand be forgotten, if a hundred times over I remember thee not...."

At 9:40 in the evening we landed in our mother country, in Pulkovo. Already that same day my novice and I reached the Novgorodian land, and our little village of Bronnitsa, from which the Holy Land seems farther than east of the sun and west of the moon, and at the same time closer than the threshold of my cell. "Greetings to you, blessed remembrances ... !"

When a person has once visited the Holy Land, it becomes near and dear to his heart forever, a second homeland (after the place of his birth), and a prefiguration of the Heavenly Fatherland....

Here, the memory of that unforgettable and awaited sojourn lifts one's thoughts on high, and fills the heart with inexpressible joy, ineffable gratitude, and everlasting love in the Lord.

Blessed is the Lord God, Who has granted me a sinner the happiness of setting foot on this God-chosen Land, and to touch its holy places with my heart.⁶

In concluding his description of the unforgettable impressions from his blessed pilgrimage, Father Ilarion delivers an ardent address "to all Christians of the Novgorod Diocese, to all believing and non-believing people living in the Novgorod Region and beyond, to old and young, men and women, and first and foremost to the younger generation, which is to build the Russia of the future."

> Naturally ... there is no better way of encountering the desired land than to visit it, prayerfully revering all its holy places ... to go amid the places of our Savior's sorrows and His glory, His crucifixion and resurrection, there to directly and more deeply experience and realize the meaning beyond all understanding of these holy places for each Christian, where our salvation was accomplished; to delve into the inexhaustible sources of divine grace, which abundantly flows out of this land ... to see with one's own eyes the miracle of the descent of the Divine Fire from heaven and the fiery sea of flame in the church, dispelling the darkness of ignorance and confirming in the faith; to experience the holy ecstasy that accompanies this great miracle. All this enraptures and ignites the soul with a bright inner flame, making an unforgettable impression upon it.[7]

Now, after Father's repose, the feelings and thoughts embodied in his address, which reflect the loftiness of his God-enlightened soul, take on a special significance. They move one to bow down in reverence before the magnitude of his pastoral spirit, guiding his readers' hearts to the work of their salvation and responding to the most pressing questions regarding the purpose and meaning of earthly human life.

> After the final service in the Holy Land,
>
> at the entrance to Trinity Cathedral at the Russian Mission
>
> ... It is time for us to go. Submitting to God's will, we set sail ....
>
> Farewell, beloved, desired Jerusalem, most holy city ....
>
> Let my right hand be forgotten, if a hundred times over I remember thee not ....

"The Holy Land now lies behind me, and before me the sea surges and crashes, like our life upon the earth."

We share here a detailed review of *In the Promised Land* by Archimandrite Ilarion (Prikhodko), written on the occasion of his 80th birthday.[8]

"I have been given a fresh copy of the book *In the Promised Land*, published in a very small run by the Boomerang firm in Veliky Novgorod. Perhaps there are some who have not read it? It is an amazing publication. The author is a man of God. He possesses a clear, sincere style, broad knowledge, an awed heart, rich life experience, and profound faith in the Lord. He would have all men live in purity of soul and righteousness. Being imperfect, however, he was drawn into various vanities.

"In order to replenish his spiritual strength, in 1999 Archimandrite Ilarion left the little village of Bronnitsa, in Novgorod, to make a pilgrimage of great difficulty, on Holy Week, to the Holy Land. 'It is farther away'—the author begins his 'edifying tale'—'than east of the sun and west of the moon, and at the same time closer than the threshold of my cell. When a person has once visited the Holy Land, it becomes near and dear to his heart forever, a second homeland (after the place of his birth), and a prefiguration of the Heavenly Fatherland.' The reader's imagination is instantly captivated upon reading the very first page, and is not released until the end. One senses that the author was writing in a state of high emotion and excitement, reliving 'those holy minutes, those blessed days.'

"We enter Palestine along with Father Ilarion, hearing the sound of our own footsteps 'along narrow cobblestone streets.' We look around in astonishment and see into the distant past, which shows through visibly in craftsmen's workshops and medieval buildings. Today it is 'a crowd of people careening in an unstoppable, variegated, multilingual stream: curious tourists hung about with cameras, loudly exchanging rich jokes; exotic rows of countless oriental trade stalls, upon entering which Russian Christians rub their eyes in astonishment: how many priceless treasures removed from Russia have found their way here!' We physically perceive both the country's flavor and the aggressive, forceful rhythm of the new century, where market relations dictate their own rules of the game. To the market, truly nothing is sacred.

"The impression given is that this is no hoary-headed man who has taken pen in hand, but an inquisitive youth, who examines the world and the faces around him with interest, not omitting a single detail. To him, everything is important, valuable, and useful. The result is that, when you finish, you have read not a traveler's log, but a serious spiritual treatise on 'the cornerstone of faith,' and the necessity of purification. The author is a true son of Russia, a patriot, whose heart brims with pain and anxiety for the fate of the people. He sees that much that is sinful has accumulated in society, and that each of us is in need of a deed performed for the sake of goodness.

"The book, in which the storyline builds gradually in emotional intensity, has several tense culminative points. One of these is the acquisition of grace-imbued strength in the pure waters of the Jordan. 'Donning a new white shirt, with deep faith in the help of God's grace ... I too, a sinner, quenched my heart's thirst in the pure streams of the Jordan. Out of sheer joy I submerged myself in its life-giving waters nine times, and felt the grace-imbued strength that helped me, infirm as I am, to surmount the entire difficult blessed journey....' These cool streams seem to touch us also. Not every person is fated to visit the Holy Land, but the inner need and longing for pure wellsprings must be preserved in the soul of every person, no matter how difficult his circumstances. In this lies the great moral mission of the author as an Orthodox person. The strength that entered his vitals gives value to every word of his preaching. He conveys this strength to believing Christians, teaching them to recognize their purpose, and not to feel themselves a mere leaf, hammered into the ground by the rain.

"In setting off on this lengthy and spiritually intensive journey, not for a moment does Father Ilarion forget his children, the parishioners of the Transfiguration of the Lord Church in the village of Bronnitsa. It is to the simple folk that he addresses his experiences, trustingly confiding his minutest shades of feeling. Drawing them along with him on his pilgrimage, on the way the rector reveals the names of his prominent fellow champions of the faith, peeling back layer after layer of their accumulated spiritual wisdom. A sorrowful book, it would seem: after all, it recounts the Lord's final journey. Yet each page glows with heartfelt warmth, and radiates with Truth.

"Now the first step is taken along the Via Dolorosa. Together with a crowd numbering in the thousands, sharing with it in a single purpose, Father traces the path which in Orthodoxy is called 'the path of martyrdom,' experiencing feelings of suffering and indelible pain. 'The procession is moving and solemn,' Father Ilarion relates, 'with candles and crosses in hand and prayerful hymns....' Following in his wake we, too, catch the scent of dampness from 'the Lord's prison cell': 'prayerfully, with heartfelt contrition and prayer that we sinful ones be forgiven, we kissed the fetters washed in the Savior's most-holy Blood.'

"Everything he experienced is trustingly passed on to us, that for but a moment the reader might be plucked from the snares of vanity, and think: why are the heights from which life's meaning is revealed so unattainable? It was our lives that the Savior's blood paid for, and yet we lose ourselves in a whirlpool of pettiness. When will we recollect ourselves? When will we start talking sense?

"Behind every page, behind every line of intense feeling, with increasing clarity a beautiful image shines through of a man ILLU-MINED, who has succeeded in infusing love into both his attitude towards people and his life, foreordained to God—bright, exalted, and noble. It appears that the Holy Fire, 'the Fire of the Holy Spirit, the Fire of salvation, the Fire of life,' to which Father Ilarion was an eyewitness, illumined and renewed his entire life. He describes the ecstasy with which he received into his hands the bundles of candles that burned, touching his face and beard without inflicting any burns whatsoever; he heard the exclamations and cries of ecstatic joy of all those present. Most importantly, however, this Holy Fire burns unceasingly in his heart.

"The rector's ardent urgings—'Let us maintain in our souls the spiritual fire of faith,' and: 'Let us not disgrace the good name of "Orthodox Christian"'—are heard by his readers, the faithful. The clergyman confirms his convictions and stances by the whole of his long life, ridding them entirely of faintheartedness and hypocrisy.

"He is magnanimous, since he has submitted himself to the laws of a spiritual thinker, who suffers only Truth.

"Involuntarily, one wonders what profound power this man possesses, who tells us with full authority: 'Let us walk in the light of Christ's commandments, like sons and daughters of the Light.' You feel a sense of deep respect and gratitude to Father Ilarion, who with such inexorable perseverance has maintained the spiritual fire of faith in our souls for so many long, difficult years. This is especially to be valued now, when values have been subverted.

"The book shows us an image of 'the Promised Land.' Its purpose is 'to reveal to the world which lies in wickedness, living in hatred and division, the salvific mystery of the sacrifice on Golgotha.' As a zealous believer and true patriot, Father Ilarion muses on what must be done so that 'the resurrection of our souls might begin,' that 'good might triumph in our hearts,' and, finally, that 'our peace of soul' might be established. His answer is unambiguous: seek the sole path for your salvation. It is a difficult path, but it must be walked. Go, in spite of hardships and grievances both from friends and from your own sinful habits.

"Power, glory, money—all this is corruption if God's grace touches a person and he experiences the wonder of the knowledge of truth on earth. This was the experience of the book's author, and he has made us also communicants of his experiences.

"In Bronnitsa, at the Transfiguration of the Lord Church, the rector is highly revered. The church parishioners and clergy are unanimous in their acknowledgement: 'All Bronnitsa is graced by Father Ilarion's selfless pastoral service to God. Here, we breathe the faith.'

"Bronnitsa, July 7, 2004."

Chronology

June 24/July 7, 1924	Archimandrite Ilarion (Ivan Fomich Prikhodko) was born in the village of Alenovka, Unechsky District, Bryansk Region.
1938	He graduated from elementary school.
1939–1941	He worked at the Unechsky railroad depot as a decorative painter.
1943	He went to war, where he was wounded. Upon returning from the front, he worked on the Alenovka communal farm.
1950	He was accepted as a novice at the Nativity of the Mother of God Men's Hermitage in Glinsk.
December 6, 1957	With the blessing of His Holiness Patriarch Alexey I, Ivan Fomich Prikhodko was tonsured a monk with the name Ilarion, in honor of Venerable Ilarion the Great.
September 3, 1959	The monk Ilarion, then a member of the brethren of the Glinsk Hermitage, was ordained to the rank of hierodeacon by Archbishop Antony of Chernigov and Nezhin.[1]

December 30, 1961	"Condescending to the increased requests of the Church Council of the Church of the Archangel Michael in the village of Borisovka, Belgorod Region," Hierodeacon Ilarion was appointed rector of the church by Bishop Leonid of Kursk and Belgorod.[2]
December 31, 1961	Hierodeacon Ilarion was ordained to the rank of hieromonk at the Divine Liturgy in the Kursk Cathedral by Bishop Leonid of Kursk and Belgorod.
March 5, 1962	In honor of Pascha, Hieromonk Ilarion, rector of the Church of the Archangel Michael, "in recognition of his fervent and beneficial service to the Church of God," was awarded the epigonation.
1963	Hieromonk Ilarion was recommended for and appointed rector of Trinity Church in the village of Murom, Chelyabinsk District, Belgorod Region.
1963–1967	Hieromonk Ilarion studied at Leningrad Theological Seminary, from which he graduated, and in 1967, he was accepted as a student at Leningrad Theological Academy.
September 19, 1967	Following the repose of Metropolitan Nikodim of Leningrad and Ladoga,[3] fourth-year Leningrad Theological Seminary alumnus Hieromonk Ilarion was presented with the esteemed award of a pectoral cross by the Holy Synod.
1971	Hieromonk Ilarion graduated Leningrad Theological Academy with a PhD in theology. The title of his thesis was "New Testament and Patristic Teaching on the Sacrament of Repentance."

1971–1973	He lived among the brethren of the Trinity-Sergius Lavra.
1973	After expulsion for not being registered with the Trinity-Sergius Lavra, he was appointed as the priest of the Church of the Holy Apostle Philip in Novgorod on July 19, then elevated the same year to the rank of hegumen.
October 6, 1975	Hieromonk Hilarion was relieved of his duties as priest at the Church of the Holy Apostle Philip and appointed rector of the Transfiguration of the Lord Church in the village of Bronnitsa, Novgorod Region Region.
April 25, 1976	Hegumen Ilarion was awarded the palitza by order of the Holy Synod and on the recommendation of Metropolitan Nikodim of Novgorod and Leningrad.
April 2, 1980	By order of the Holy Synod and on the recommendation of Metropolitan Antony of Novgorod and Leningrad, Hegumen Ilarion was awarded the jeweled cross in honor of Holy Pascha.
February 13, 1981	By order of the Holy Synod and on the recommendation of Metropolitan Antony of Novgorod and Leningrad, Hegumen Ilarion was elevated to the rank of archimandrite "for zealous service to the Church of God." The ordination was performed during the All-night Vigil in the Church of the Holy Apostle Philip on the Feast of the Holy Hierarch Nikita of Novgorod.
February 16, 1981	Archimandrite Ilarion was appointed confessor of the Novgorod Diocese.

1987   In honor of the Feast of Holy Pascha, "for longstanding and zealous service to the Church of God," Archimandrite Ilarion was honored with the right to serve the Divine Liturgy with the royal doors open until the Cherubic Hymn.

1988   "In recognition of ecclesiastical merit and in honor of the 30th anniversary of his ordination," Archimandrite Ilarion was made a member of the Russian Orthodox Church's Order of the Holy Equal-to-the-Apostles Great Prince Vladimir of the Third Rank.

1990   "For fervent and zealous service to the Church of God," Archimandrite Ilarion was awarded the right to serve the Divine Liturgy with the royal doors open until the prayer Our Father.

1994   On the recommendation of Bishop Lev of Novgorod and Staraya Russa, "for fervent service to the Church of God and in honor of his 70th birthday," His Holiness Patriarch Alexis II of Moscow and All Russia awarded Archimandrite Ilarion the right to wear a second jeweled pectoral cross.

1999   "In recognition of his fervent service and in honor of his 75th jubilee," His Holiness Patriarch Alexis II of Moscow and All Russia awarded Archimandrite Ilarion the Russian Orthodox Church's Order of Venerable Sergius of Radonezh of the Third Rank. During Holy Week, he made a pilgrimage to the Holy Land.

2001	He wrote the book *In the Promised Land: An Edifying Account of a Pilgrimage to the Holy City of Jerusalem and Other Holy Places* (Veliky Novgorod, Russia: Boomerang).
2004	"In recognition of his fervent service and in honor of his 80th jubilee," His Holiness Patriarch Alexis II of Moscow and All Russia awarded Archimandrite Ilarion the Russian Orthodox Church's Order of the Holy Equal-to-the-Apostles Great Prince Vladimir of the Second Rank.
May 29, 2008	He reposed and was buried in Veliky Novgorod in the Barlaam of Khutyn Monastery, near the altar of the Transfiguration Cathedral.

Liturgical Texts for the Glinsk Icon of the Most-Holy Mother of God

TROPARION

Tone 4

Today right-believing people,

overshadowed by the holy image of the Mother of God, say with compunction:

O Lady, help Thy servants amid dangers, sorrows, and sickness, burdened with many sins,

and deliver us from every evil,

praying to Thy Son, Christ our God, that He save our souls.

KONTAKION

Tone 8

Though Thine icon wast many times carried off from the place of its appearance, O Mother of God,

yet more wondrously did it return to the hermitage,

from whence it bestoweth things good and needful on all the faithful.

MEGALYNARION

We magnify Thee,

O Most-Holy Virgin,

and we honor Thy holy image,

by which Thou dost heal our pains

and dost raise up our souls to God.

Memorial Verses

Beholding my grave, remember my love. . . .

The following are verses written by Father Ilarion's spiritual children after his repose.

> This elder, our God-given leader,
> Our father and our mother is,
> In love to serve Christ was he called,
> And read'ly makes each person his.
>
> Peace of soul for ill and aged,
> Shelter o'er the orphan's head,
> Model for those weak in spirit,
> Those by worldly cares beset!
>
> His love is boundless; to all men
> All things our father does become.
> Before him proud men bow their heads,
> And wise men are not deaf, but dumb.
>
> Here love pervades the very air,
> An elder's love—our father's care.
> All blooms and ripens 'neath his gaze,
> Like fruit beneath the sunlight rays![1]

***

Our sunshine leaves us, fading to the west
On this day of sadness.
We have wept until no tears remain.
Where are you, our gladness?

From confinement has he been delivered,
from flesh and blood's travail.
He has come out of imprisonment
In this earthly vale.

Unto his remembrance everlasting
Goes our righteous one, our joy unfading
The best of memorials he leaves us:
Life within his children's souls unwaning.

Handmaid of God, A.

***

You taught us that there is no death,
That love never will pass away,
That in our window shines only one Light,
By whom everything blooms day to day.

On earth you lived for heaven alone,
Spurning flatt'ry and glory's deception,
And for you people's hearts long daily:
For them, you were salvation's inception.

Anonymous spiritual child

***

Our helmsman he was, not just one of the crew,
Over waves, by the stormy sea tossed.
A wise man, gray-headed, our guide to the harbor
Of God's divine purpose for us.

He was our father, our mother as well,
A physician appointed by God,
Demanding that all of us put off our shoes
As His most-pure threshold we trod.

And today, on the day of your angel,
Taming the internal storm,
To you, Father, mem'ry eternal
We sing, as a choir we form.

Anonymous spiritual child

***

The sun has disappeared from sight; the grass has turned
    to blue . . .
How, Ilarionushka, has your life gone out?
As a boy, Vanyushenka, 'cross meadows did you run,
Ever seeking in your little soul God's holy church.
To Glinsk, to the monastery led your winding road,
And the Psalter did you study, to draw close to God.
As a young ascetic six years did you serve,
And this house together with its elders came to love.
To the Holy Land the young boy always dreamed to go,
For at least a little while, if only in a dream.
And to the Lord did he depart, finding joy at last,
By the Holy Spirit sated, like a babe with milk.
This radiant joy of faith cannot be killed by any means;
Sorrows, persecutions, grief—all this it survived.
This torch will not be smothered by our earthly gloom—
In our wintry Novgorod the sun has now set.
Over thirty years the elder served in our small town,
Instructing in wisdom people young and old.
Our God loves the righteous, giving Love for Love.
One who trusts in God is prepared to give Him all.
In the Holy Land our Father did sojourn,
And in mem'ry of himself he left to us his book.
Our caring, loving Father we never will forget,
With whose holy love pure hearts continually
    are filled.

Anonymous spiritual child, May 31, 2008

***

Jesus, Giver of life, pray attend
To the prayer of Your unworthy children.
Illumine our Father with Light uncreated,
Give him rest in a place of green pasture.

Living not for himself, on his shoulders he bore us,
Not thinking it too great a load.
In his pastoral heart did he carry away
The great chronicle listing our sins.

We offer You thanks with all of our heart
For Your gift, for your infinite mercy.
You will not fault him for ardor of soul,
For his heart, rendered contrite by weeping . . . ?

The candle is snuffed, the soul has now flown,
And our great man of prayer is extinguished.
But look down from heaven on all us who pray,
And hark to the voice of his children:

Help us in love ever closer to grow,
Avoiding all strife and contention.
And may Father's works be shown forth in that place
Where the saints ever sing: *Alleluia.*

There by Your breath flowers burst into bloom,
And heavenly birds sing their songs.
There is no sorrow, pain, evil, or grief,
Only life and love, ever prolonged.

Anonymous spiritual child

***

For God's sake you forsook the world,
And to heaven leads your only road.

Anonymous spiritual child

***

O Lord, our Lord, to Thee do I pray:
All heaven's sweetness Thy servant vouchsafe . . .

Anonymous spiritual child

***

To you in much-loved Bronnitsa
The wave of people does not go.
But zealously it surges toward
Your relics, in the earth preserved.

And there, before the mound, souls offer
Fervent prayers of grief and sorrow
Up to heaven, confidently
Hoping on the help to follow.

Anonymous spiritual child

***

Come to me, come to me still closer,
From beneath the earth we hear a voice.
Come and kiss, come and kiss most gently
My Faith, my Steadfast hope, and my great Love.

Anonymous spiritual child

***

Everything passes, yet everything stays,
And inscribed on the soul's fervent scroll remains.

Anonymous spiritual child

***

A memory sacred lives on in our hearts,
By name—*Ilarion*.
The time may go by, but it will not erase
The things that he built as from stone.

Anonymous spiritual child

***

Our pain never ceasing
Cannot be relinquished.
Could the soul be more cut to the quick?
Both today and tomorrow
In faith will we stand
And mem'ry eternal will sing:
Memory eternal,
Memory eternal,
Memory eternal . . .

Anonymous spiritual child

Beholding my grave, remember my love. . . .

NOTES

The author followed a Russian cultural and intellectual practice in which it is not considered necessary to cite all sources fully, if at all. Therefore the endnotes are listed to facilitate the reader's understanding.

From the Preface to the Russian Language Edition
1. Blessed Augustine.
2. 1 Cor 2:15.
3. Ps 112:6.
4. Rom 8:35, 37–39.
5. *The Rudder*, 1803, No. 23.
6. Matt 3:2–3.

Chapter 1
1. Nun Evlampia lived in a village neighboring Alenovka. She was a prudent woman and clairvoyant. Father Ilarion regarded her with great respect, heeded her words, and asked her advice in all matters.

2. T. Kulpinova, *The Bronnitsa Outpost* (no.1; Sophia, 1977), 11–2.

3. Father Ilarion had a great love for Victory Day. Each year on May 9, moved by his sacred duty to pray for the soldiers who had laid down their lives for their faith, their fatherland, and their people, tormented in captivity and in concentration camps, who had ended their lives amid suffering in the wars of our own times, he served memorial services in the Bronnitsa church. He always

reminded others that the Fascists had invaded "our" land on June 22, 1941, on the day of All Saints of Russia, and that World War II ended when the Church was celebrating the Pascha of Christ, when in restored churches, the paschal greeting "Christ is risen" ended in the exclamation "Greetings with the victory!" The people's faith in the risen Christ resurrected our deeply suffering homeland. Through faith, Father Ilarion aroused and enrooted in us a love for our fatherland, which he wanted to see as a strong, morally powerful country to be reckoned with.

4. Hieroschemamonk Gabriel was cell attendant to Father Seraphim (Amelin) after the monastery opened, and Father Andronik was his spiritual father. All who spent time in the hermitage in those days lovingly remembered him as a dependable treasurer and provisor and, most importantly, a profound man of prayer. When he died, Father Seraphim (Romantsev), the monastery superior, said, "Half the monastery died with Father Gabriel" (Schema-Archimandrite Ioann [Maslov], *The Glinsk Paterikon* [Moscow: Samshit, 1997], 605–7). Later, in Novgorod, Father Ilarion said in one of his sermons, "Perhaps you think that today there are no ascetics like those of old. This is not true. When I was living in the Glinsk Hermitage, there was a hieromonk, Gabriel, a man of great spirit and pious life."

Chapter 2

1. Archimandrite Makary (Glukhov).

2. Schema-Archimandrite Ioann (Maslov), *The Glinsk Hermitage: A History of the Hermitage and Its Work of Spiritual Enlightenment in the XIV–XX Centuries* (Moscow: Publishing Division of the Moscow Patriarchate, 1994), 497.

3. Ibid., 477.

4. As testified in *The Glinsk Paterikon*, Brother Vlasy was a tremendous worker. In addition to many other obediences, in his love and compassion for people, he undertook the labor of exorcising the possessed (many spiritual fathers in the Glinsk Hermitage performed exorcisms). Both he and Hieromonk Ilarion, by order of the commissary of affairs of the Russian

Orthodox Church and the corresponding order of Archbishop Andrei (Sukhenko), administrator of the Sumsk Diocese, would be dismissed from the Glinsk Hermitage even before it was closed, in early April 1961. Brother Vlasy continued his service to God and neighbor at St Barbara Church in the city of Tbilisi, where he died in 1989. For a time, he lived in a monastery in Odessa, from which Father Ilarion received this congratulatory telegram from him, dated November 4, 1982: "Dear Father Ilarion, congratulations on your nameday. I wish you health, salvation, and all God's mercies. Archimandrite Vlasy."

5. Father Ilarion seemed to be grafted to this name. Venerable Ilarion the Great was born in A.D. 291 in Palestine, near the city of Gaza. He was buried in Cyprus, but his relics were later moved to his native country. During his pilgrimage to the Holy Land, Father Ilarion visited the cave church dedicated to Venerable Ilarion. Archimandrite Ilarion described this visit with considerable emotion in his book *In the Promised Land: An Edifying Account of a Pilgrimage to the Holy City of Jerusalem and Other Holy Places* (Veliky, Novgorod: Boomerang, 2003): "The visit to this cave caught my heart up into the greatest spiritual joy. With reverence and profound prayer I fell down before the altar of the saint. My gladness of spirit was the greater in that this unexpected joy occurred on Great Wednesday, on the great feast of the Annunciation of the Most-Holy Mother of God" (63).

6. Schema-Archimandrite Ioann (Maslov), *The Glinsk Paterikon*, 8.

7. Pers. comm., June 24, 2008.

8. In his sermons on the celebration of the wonder-working image and on the Tuesday of Bright Week, Father Ilarion always recounted its history in detail. When in Moscow, he never failed to visit the Church of the Resurrection of Christ in Sokolniki, praying with reverence to the Good Gatekeeper and humbly praying before Her most-pure image for help in every need. At the end of October 1999, when an exact copy of the Wonder-Working Icon of the Hebron Mother of God was brought to Moscow from the Holy Mount Athos and placed in the Moscow Church of the

Dormition of the Most-Holy Mother of God in Trinity-Lykovo (Strogino), Father Ilarion traveled there despite his infirmity, and his joy knew no bounds.

9. *The Glinsk Mosaic: Pilgrims' Recollections of the Glinsk Hermitage (1942–1961)* (Moscow: Pilgrim, 1997), 35–6.

10. "The River Dnieper" is a Ukranian folk song.

11. Ibid., 41–2.

12. Archimandrite Raphael (Karelin), *On the Path from Time to Eternity: Recollections* (Saratov, Russia: Saratov Diocese Publishing, 2008), 555.

13. Ibid., 182.

14. Ibid.

15. Ibid., 182–3.

16. Ibid., 183.

17. Iveron is what was then the Soviet Republic of Georgia.

18. Ibid., 232.

19. The Cell Rule of Five Hundred is a private office of monastic origin which includes the recitation five hundred times of the Jesus Prayer: "Lord Jesus Christ, Son of God, have mercy on me, a sinner."

20. Father Raphael (Karelin) cited an instance when a certain hieromonk asked Archimandrite Seraphim about a hermit who constantly imagined the faces of Christ and the saints. In answer to his question as to whether salvation is possible when someone prays this way, Father Seraphim replied,

> Whether he will be saved or not, I do not know, but it is impossible to reach high degrees through improper prayerful activity. The imagination is a quality of the soul, not the spirit, and is linked to the passions. The Holy Fathers compare this kind of prayer with darkness in the dead of night. A person does not know where he is going; he is buffeted by his enemy, but cannot retaliate or even dodge them. . . . Imagining the spiritual world can arouse a feeling of secret pride in a person: it begins to seem to him that he is really seeing this world during prayer. Many of those who have fallen into spiritual delusion prayed in this

way. In any case, if this hermit is not spiritually deluded he is certainly on a dangerous path. (*Selected Essays*, 561–2)

21. Noted Father Raphael, "The Glinsk elders used to say that a monk who is a fornicator is Judas' brother: Judas betrayed Christ, the Second Hypostasis of the Holy Trinity, and the fornicator betrays the Third Hypostasis of the Divinity—the Holy Spirit. The elders said that the children of monks are usually born ill, and their progeny die out by the second or third generation" (*Selected Essays*, 567).

Chapter 3

1. The office of Father Ilarion's cell attendant was held at various times by Mothers Tatiana Emelianovna, Vera Prosvetova, Alexandra Mishchenko, Anna Krasovskaya, and Valentina Bondarenko.

2. Record, 2008.

3. 2 Tim 2:9.

4. *On the Life of Schema-Archimandrite Vitaly: Recollections of His Spiritual Children, Letters, and Teachings* (Moscow: New Savior Monastery, 2002), 60.

5. Archimandrite Raphael (Karelin), *On the Path from Time to Eternity*, 204.

6. Ibid., 190.

7. Ibid., 205.

8. Ibid.

9. A hegumen is typically the head of a monastery, but the title can be awarded honorifically to any hieromonk.

10. Schema-Archimandrite Ioann (Maslov), *The Glinsk Hermitage*, 468.

11. *On the Life of Schema-Archimandrite Vitaly*, 70.

Chapter 5

1. *Elder Archimandrite Seraphim (Tyapochkin) of Belgorod, 1894–1982: Life, Recollections of His Spiritual Children, and Sermons* (Moscow: Church of Sophia the Divine Wisdom, Tradeservice, 2006), 3. Many believers heard of Father Seraphim in connection

with the memorable "Zoya's standing," which occurred in Samara (then Kuibyshev) in 1956. Father Seraphim (Hieromonk Dimitry at the time) was involved in the occurrence, which shook the entire Orthodox world. It was he who succeeded, after fervent and ardent prayer, in removing the icon of Saint Nicholas from the stiffened hands of the literally petrified girl, who had gone to a dance and there danced with the icon during the Nativity Fast. Father Seraphim said at the time, "Now we must wait for a sign on the Great Day of Christ" (i.e., Pascha), and so it came to pass.

2. *Elder Archimandrite Seraphim (Tyapochkin) of Belgorod, 1894–1982*, 3.

Chapter 6

1. Vladyka Prokl studied at the Leningrad Theological Seminary at the time when Father Ilarion was serving there as Dean.

2. Archpriest Vladimir Ustinovich Sorokin (village of Zlynka, Maloviskinsky Region, Kirovograd Region, March 5, 1939–) graduated from the Leningrad Theological Academy in 1965. He served as an archpriest, a professor, and the rector of the Leningrad (as of 1991, the St Petersburg) Theological Academy and Seminary from August 22, 1987, to August 12, 1992. Since 2009 he has served as the rector of Prince Vladimir Cathedral in St Petersburg.

3. Professor Archpriest Vladimir Sorokin, ed., *Succession* (St Petersburg, Russia: Saint Vladimir Cathedral, 2007), 3.

4. Ibid, 101–2.

5. It was to repent that he first left worldly life and entered a monastery.

6. 2 Tim 3:12.

Chapter 7

1. Archimandrite Augustine (Nikitin), *Metropolitan Nikodim of Novgorod (1967–1978)* (no. 3; Bucharest, Romania: Sophia, 2008), 40.

2. Ibid., 39–40.

3. Ibid., 40.

4. Ibid.

5. Pers. comm., February 2009.

6. Father Ilarion deeply revered the Russian land's cherished Vladimir Icon of the Mother of God, keeping its feasts both on August 26/September 8, in commemoration of Russia's deliverance from being destroyed by the Mongol Tatars, and on June 23/July 6, in commemoration of Russia's deliverance from Khan Ahmat of the Mongol Horde in 1480, as well as Moscow's miraculous deliverance from the Crimean Khan Mahmet Girei in 1521.

Chapter 8

1. Phil 1:21, 23.

2. This is a euphemism for the local office of the KGB.

3. The time of unlimited freedom and permissiveness would come later. Father Ilarion required great spiritual strength and courage to remain a faithful keeper of patristic legacy and holy tradition, and to remain a faithful ideal of Holy Russia.

4. She was indeed a nun.

5. This is a method of treating alcoholism.—Trans.

6. St Cyprian of Carthage, *The Unity of the Catholic Church* 6, 1st ed. (A.D. 251).

7. From the poem by Vladimir Solovev, "*Bednyy drug, istomil tebya put.*"—Trans.

8. This is an Orthodox liturgical prayer used at least once in every service and in the rule of morning and evening prayers, outside of the paschal season.

9. Metropolitan Veniamin (Fedchenkov), *On Belief, Unbelief, and Doubt* (Moscow: Ruslo, 1992), 79. It should be noted that Vladyka Veniamin's memoirs concern the former, prerevolutionary Church. Our experiences are closely linked to our father, Archimandrite Ilarion, and hence, thanks be to God, pertain to the time when he was with us.

10. In the original there was yet another verse:

And our Father, our dearly beloved one,

By the prayers of the Most-Holy Mother—
Long may He live, and God's Kingdom receive,
in good health one year after another.

11. 2 Cor 12:9.

12. Gennady Ivanov, pers. comm.

13. Anna Z., pers. comm.

14. Pers. comm.

15. Pers. comm.

16. Pers. comm.

17. Ps 103:15.

18. *A Spiritual Treasury Gathered from Earth*.

19. Phil 1:23–25.

20. Ps 57:7.

21. Holy Hierarch John, Archbishop of Shanghai and San Francisco.

22. Saint Tikhon of Zadonsk.

23. Job 42:17.

24. John 10:7.

25. *Tolkovaya Bibliya* [Bible with Commentary] (book 3, vol. 9; 1912; repr. Stockholm: 1987), 370, 410, 412.

26. John 9:5.

27. *Tolkovaya Bibliya*, 410.

28. John 10:1–10.

29. John 10:9.

30. Sir 41:1 (*The Orthodox Study Bible*).

31. 1 Thess 4:13.

32. The future appeared to Father Ilarion as "the substance of things hoped for" (Heb 11:1). He taught us also to "love the eternal church, the Heavenly church, where there will be eternal sun, where there will be neither sadness nor sighing, where the Lord Himself will illumine and warm us and give us life, joy, and blessedness. But for this we must pass through the furnace of our earthly life, with the help of the Lord and the Mother of God" (from one of his sermons).

33. 1 Cor 13:8.

34. Venerable Macarius of the Altai is commemorated May 18/31. On this day, the holy fathers of the seven ecumenical counsels are likewise commemorated. According to *The Glinsk Paterikon* (Schema-Archimandrite Ioann [Maslov], 148–50), Archimandrite Macarius (Glukharev; 1792–1847) was an alumnus of the Glinsk Hermitage, a worthy disciple of its superior, Abbot Philaret (Danilevsky), and the founder of the Altai Ecclesiastical Mission.

Chapter 9
1. Josh 23:14.
2. John 11:11.
3. John 11:14.
4. Rom 5:14.
5. Rom 5:8.
6. Rom 5:10.
7. 1 Cor 15:22.
8. Rev 14:13.

Chapter 10
1. Pers. comm.
2. Pers. comm.
3. Pers. comm.
4. Pers. comm.
5. Pers. comm.
6. Pers. comm.
7. Pers. comm.
8. Pers. comm.
9. *Novgorodskie Vedomosti* [Novgorod Journal], May 31, 2008.
10. John 17:12.

Chapter 11
1. Prov 4:18.
2. Holy Hierarch Luke (Voino-Yasenetsky), *Science and Religion: Spirit, Soul, and Body* (Rostov-on-Don, Rostov Region, Russia: Troitskoe Slovo, 2001), 275–9.

3. Prov 4:18.
4. 1 Cor 4:15.
5. Phil 3:13–14.
6. Col 4:5.
7. 1 Cor 7:29.
8. John 9:4.
9. Gal 5:22–23.
10. Saint John Climacus, *The Ladder of Divine Ascent*, Step 9, 16.
11. 1 Cor 12:8.
12. In his book *Three Talks on the Church*, Metropolitan Anthony of Sourozh cited an excellent example that also sheds light on Father Ilarion's approach to this issue. Once, Metropolitan Anthony was approached by a certain clergyman. In answer to all of Vladyka Anthony's questions—whether he wanted lemon, whether he took sugar or jam in his tea, and so forth—the cleric responded, "As you bless." At last, Vladyka Anthony could stand it no longer and said, "I bless you to speak the truth."
13. Gal 5:23; 1 Tim 1:9.
14. Mark 10:43.

Chapter 12

1. Titus 2:14.
2. Saint John of Kronstadt, *Thoughts of an Orthodox Christian on Repentance and Holy Communion* (Moscow: Synodal Library, 1990), 00.
3. Troparion of the 9th Ode.
4. Canon of Saint Andrew of Crete
5. Rev 5:6.
6. 1 Cor 2:13.
7. 1 Thess 5:17–18.
8. Sir 35:17 (*The Orthodox Study Bible*).
9. Pers. comm., September 2008.

Chapter 13

1. A reference to an untitled poem by Alexander Pushkin.—Trans.

2. Some last names have been forgotten.

3. Schema-Archimandrite Ioann [Maslov], *The Glinsk Paterikon*, 460.

4. Ibid., 455.

5. Ibid., 684.

6. Heb 5:8–9.

7. Schema-Archimandrite Ioann [Maslov], *The Glinsk Paterikon*, 509.

8. Luke 6:34.

9. Luke 6:34–35.

10. Matt 5:1–5, 14–15, 18.

11. Holy Righteous John of Kronstadt.

Chapter 14

1. Rom 5:3.

2. Eph 6:12.

3. As Archimandrite Pavel (Gruzdev) noted, "When a monk skips, everyone sees. When a monk weeps, no one perceives."

4. Father found particular joy, as he himself once said, in baptizing children in the church.

5. Sir 2:1 (*The Orthodox Study Bible*).

6. Job 2:10, 1:21 (*The Orthodox Study Bible*).

7. Apparently, Father Ilarion adhered to the Gospel saying, "In the mouth of two or three witnesses every word may be established" (Matt 18:16).

8. Schema-Archimandrite Ioann [Maslov], *The Glinsk Paterikon*, 504.

9. Nikolai Minsky.

10. Matt 11:29.

11. 1 Cor 9:22.

12. Archimandrite Sophrony (Sakharov), *Spiritual Conversations* (vol. 1; XXX: Palomink, 2003), 224–5.

13. Archimandrite Sophrony, *Saint Silouan the Athonite* (Essex, England: Patriarchal and Stavropegic Monastery of Saint John the Baptist, 1991), 204.

14. Saint Gregory the Theologian.

15. Jas 1:27.

16. Matt 5:13–14.

17. Matt 5:16.

18. Matt 5:15.

19. 1 Cor 13:1.

20. 1 John 4:16.

21. Archimandrite Sophrony (Sakharov), *Spiritual Conversations*, 223.

22. 1 Cor 13:8.

23. 1 Pet 4:8, 10.

24. Schema-Archimandrite Ioann (Maslov), *The Glinsk Hermitage*, 495.

Chapter 15

1. Matt 18:12–13.

2. Heb 6:11–12.

3. Matt 9:12.

4. Jas 5:14–15.

5. Mark 6:7, 12–13.

6. Rom 14:17.

7. No. 272/15a.

8. T. Kulpinova, *The Bronnitsa Outpost*, 12.

9. 1 Pet 4:8, 10.

10. This prayer was first printed in France in 1912 in the spiritual magazine *La Clochette (The Little Bell)* and was attributed to Saint Francis of Assisi.

Chapter 16

1. *Sophia*.

2. By some accounts, Saint Simon was crucified for preaching the Christian faith in Georgia at the command of King Aderki, and by others in Persia.

3. The Holy Hierarch John Chrysostom, persecuted for his denunciation of social vices, was exiled to Armenia, from where he was sent to Pitiunt (now Pitsunda), but died along the way in Comana on September 14, 407.

4. Saint Nina spent the final months of her earthly life in the small town of Bodbe, in a hut on a mountainside, which after her repose came to be called "the wailing cliff." In the church, a cross plaited from a grapevine is preserved, which the Most-Holy Virgin herself presented to her when sending her to Iberia (Georgia) to preach the good news of the Gospel of the Lord Jesus Christ. Upon awakening from a light sleep and finding the cross in her hands, Saint Nina watered it with tears of joy and, cutting off her braided hair, bound the cross with it.

5. To this day, the grace-imbued stone of the venerable one, called "the stone of humility," is preserved in the church and exudes miracles. In his book *In the Promised Land*, Father Ilarion told the story

> of a certain person who all his life longed to go to Jerusalem, fasted, prayed, communed, and finally towards the end of his life set off on the journey he so ardently desired. Upon approaching the Savior's city, overcome with emotion, he knelt and prayed reverently for a long time. Then, feeling that he was unworthy to tread this holy ground with his sinful feet, he took three stones from the city wall as a memento and turned back again. That night the Angel of the Lord appeared before His Holiness Elias, Patriarch of Jerusalem, and informed him that a holy man of God who had come to Jerusalem to worship had taken back with him all the grace of the Lord's Tomb, which lay in three stones, and was carrying them home with him in a basket to Iberia. He was to be overtaken and made to return two of the stones, but permitted to take one with him. . . . This humble man was the great Georgian saint, Venerable David Garejeli. (67)

6. In ancient times, this icon was a symbol of Byzantium and was kept in the Blachernae church in Constantinople. Seventy years before the imperial capital fell, however, the icon disappeared and was found in Rus', and later ended up in the United States.

Chapter 17

1. This is a reference to the Russian fairy tale "Masha and the Bear," in which a little girl escapes from captivity in the home of a bear by stowing away in a basket of cakes, which he has agreed to take to her parents. Each time the bear wishes to sit down and eat a cake, the girl warns him not to in these quoted words, and the bear is amazed, supposing that she can still see him from the house.—Trans.

Chapter 18

1. Archimandrite Ilarion, *In the Promised Land*, 11.
2. Ibid., 12.
3. From the poem "Peterburg" by Boris Pasternak.—Trans.
4. Archimandrite Ilarion, *In the Promised Land*, 7–10.
5. Ibid.
6. Ibid.
7. Ibid., 219.
8. This review, discovered among Father Ilarion's papers, was unsigned.

Appendix 1

1. Vladyka Antony (Melnikov) served as the Metropolitan of Leningrad and Novgorod after 1978.
2. Vladyka Leonid (Polyakov, 1913–1990) was born in St Petersburg. He worked as a doctor until 1949, when he was ordained a deacon and served at the front. He graduated from the Leningrad Theological Academy in 1952 as a candidate of theology, and received the tonsure at the Pskov Caves Monastery, taking the name Leonid. Ordained a presbyter in 1955, he served as an assistant professor at the Leningrad Theological Academy and as the dean of students at the Moscow Theological Academy. Consecrated bishop of Kursk and Belgorod in 1959, he then became archbishop of Riga and Latvia in 1966. In 1979, he became a metropolitan. He is buried at the Transfiguration of the Lord Hermitage in Riga.
3. Metropolitan Nikodim (Boris Georgievich Rotov) was born in the village of Frolovo, Korablinsk District, Ryazan Region

on October 15, 1929, and died on on September 5, 1978, while attending the installation of Pope John Paul I at the Vatican. He received the monastic tonsure on August 19, 1947, and was ordained a hieromonk on November 20, 1949. He graduated from the Leningrad Theological Academy in 1955. On February 25, 1956, he became a member of the Russian Ecclesiastical Mission in Jerusalem, then became its head on September 25, 1957. On March 31, 1957, he was made a hegumen, and later was made an archimandrite on November 2, 1957. On June 4, 1959, he became vice chairman of the Department of Foreign Religious Affairs, and from May 31, 1960, to May 30, 1972, he served as chairman. On July 10, 1960, he was consecrated as a bishop of Podolsk and vicar of the Moscow Diocese. On November 23, 1960, he became bishop of Yaroslavl and Rostov, then the archbishop on June 10, 1961, and a metropolitan on August 3, 1963. On August 4, 1963, he was named as a metropolitan of Minsk and Belarus, then as a metropolitan of Leningrad and Ladoga on October 9, 1963, On October 7, 1967, he was also named as a metropolitan of Novgorod. As a simultaneous position, he became Patriarchal Exarch of Western Europe on September 3, 1974. He received his doctorate of theology from Leningrad Theological Academy on February 6, 1975. On May 30, 1972, he was appointed as the chairman of the Commission of the Holy Synod on Issues of Christian Unity and Interchurch Affairs. He is buried at the Alexander Nevsky Lavra cemetery.

Appendix 3

1. Mother Anna, cell attendant 34. Archimandrite Ilarion, *In the Promised Land*, 209–10.

INDEX